Benjamin Groff Herre

Hyperborea

Or, The Pilgrims of the Pole

Benjamin Groff Herre

Hyperborea
Or, The Pilgrims of the Pole

ISBN/EAN: 9783743340633

Manufactured in Europe, USA, Canada, Australia, Japa

Cover: Foto ©ninafisch / pixelio.de

Manufactured and distributed by brebook publishing software (www.brebook.com)

Benjamin Groff Herre

Hyperborea

HYPERBOREA:

OR,

THE PILGRIMS OF THE POLE.

BY BENJ. G. HERRE.

LANCASTER, PA.:
THE NEW ERA BOOK AND JOB PRINT.
1878.

ADVERTISEMENT.

CHIEFLY, the within poem is founded upon Dr. Kane's narrative of his Exploring Expedition to the Polar Regions; mainly in the descriptive portions, except a few episodal stories, allusion to which will not be found therein, having been first broached by himself.

LANCASTER, April 29, 1878.   THE AUTHOR.

HYPERBOREA:
Or, THE PILGRIMS OF THE POLE.

BOOK I.

INTRODUCTION.

Let us yet sing, the while the theme invites,
The pilgrims of the pole. Ye muses, ye
That seldom have indwelt the extreme north,
Will ye accompany? My verse invokes
Your timely and your never-faltering aid.
 First of the numerous list who sought that realm
Was Cabot, Venice-born, but sailing 'neath
Brittania's banner, second he alone
To the great Genoan who the new world found,
In maritime supremacy; the next
He was to sail that shore; the northern half
Of that new region was he first to touch,
To enter in, to set his foot upon.
He found it, what was never known before,
The continent: nor he disdained to seek
The frosty zone the foremost, tho' beyond
The sunnier far and undiscovered south
Invited and expanded, since he fain
Would find the north-west passage to Cathay,
To India, where all riches had their home,
The voyage to reward and commerce glad;
But, no—th' illimite waste no path would yield,

HYPERBOREA: OR, THE PILGRIMS OF THE POLE.

And turned him back to seek a milder clime.
Next Cortereal took that forward route,
Nor long delayed, by Portugal dispatched,
And left the wonted track around the cape
To th' orient's vast munificence, behind,
For this abandoned. Thrice the twain essayed,
The sanguine brothers here to penetrate,
But the remorseless Frost forbad the course,
And thrice they were repulsed with loss of life,
And stern disaster to the wearied crew,
Tho' yet so far from all the bound they sought.
    How many lives on that tremendous coast
Are forfeited, are wrecked on frozen fields,
Or pent by icy chains beyond escape,
Are chilled and famished 'mid the hungry void!
    Now does Sir Willoughby, when years have waned
The Northeast passage tempt to th' envious main,
Far 'yond the East, where cold Muscovy trends
By the Arctic shore, he pierces undeterred
To Nova Zembla's dreary solitude.
Driv'n back by th' all indomitable ice,
He thence returns part way, but now remains
Enclosed and fettered by th' Arrina's mouth,
Which Lapland owns. That stolid stream beholds
Him fade and die with all his fearless host,
But not a mortal sees, till after years,
They find them petrified, all, all, to death,
By the fierce cold o'ercome within their holds,
The gallant chief, with all his seamen's aids,
Congealed to lifelessness and changed to stone.
And Frobisher came to the rescue next.
Beyond a score of seasons circled round,
Since the last fatal cruise had bid a pause.
Three voyages he urged, and gave his name
To yonder oft unnavigable strait,
And tho' interior, yet an outer one
To many else, and ope'd where they are pent;
First grateful science entered in his quest,

And in his charge she grew to high designs.
  Then was Sir Gilbert too not slow to move.
A fond enthusiast for that Western path,
In firm belief th' inhospitable clime
He ventured to explore, and dared its rage.
What marvelous advent'rer he became,
What courage won him to the hard pursuit
Would none give credence, save that future toils
Must verify in partial phase, at least,
His stranger narrative ; nor were it meet
To follow him in all his various haps,
Since tho' so ardent he, his fruitless chase
Was rift all result th' enterprise t' enhance ;
Nor 'yond his predecessors did he go,
Nor aught attained they had not done before.
  But, Davis, thou did'st add, indeed, a germ
To the Arctic harvest, thou did'st speed beyond
Thy slower antecedents ; for the straits
Bear witness to thee and adopt thy name.
By inner Greenland, that forbidden shore,
Thou cast thy measurements around the scope,
Nor wouldst without thy data be driv'n off ;
Nor wert thou far in years behind the van.
Let not the envious hand of time malign,
Despoil these ocean worthies their just meed,
Who braved the earth's dread temp'rature sublime,
To manifest the wonders of the world ;
Nay, be forevermore their honors green,
The while the mundane territories teem.
  Inspired by all so fairly was achieved,
By steady seamanship within the age,
Now Holland, France and Denmark ardent waged
A competition for the pregnant prize.
Hispania's rivalry did urge them thus,
That held the South and deep Atlantic seas,
Sole mastery, approachless to the rest,
Or dealt strict punishment th' intruder there,
Who'd share their barter and divide their pow'r.

HYPERBOREA: OR, THE PILGRIMS OF THE POLE.

    Thus did the Netherlands too persevere,
To search the Northeast. Thence did Barnets go,
That manful sailor, tho' too ill prepared,
For the stern difficulties would beset
Him there, and overwhelm him at the last,
And which he could not have conceived at first.
Twice he recovered and his struggling crew ;
Thrice he determined, but by th' icy Cape
Of far America, by Russia held,
Did perish in the frigid boat where all
Were moored and straitened in the dangerous Frost ;
Nor was his great and hoped accomplishment,
Of precious moment or of much avail.
    Such are their perils who the doubtful maze
Of nature tempt, that wrests them from her sphere.
Oh ! what a waste of labor, doubts and fears,
Is vainly spent, that, turned to hopeful aims,
Would grow to payment ! Ah, how oft the soul
Of true endeavor hath a slight reward !
Yet is that fervor ever thrown away,
And wholly lost ? Who seeks not ne'er will find ;
Who never tries shall never know. Will not
That purpose find some soil wherein to spring;
Some fond successor, who will cultivate
The earnest root unto a useful end,
In its own period, will there not arise ?
    Whate'er the import of these oft attempts,
A century's overplus is dissipate, since
This bold divergence t'ward the Pole began.
Then Hudson, he receives command to steer
Toward the North direct. Thither he hies,
And by Spitzbergen's rigorous border wends,
But by th' impassable bound'ry soon is stopped,
Forbidden farther progress : so returns.
Now to the East he speeds, for India bound.
The ice prevails, and he must needs retrace
His briny footstep that same year he went.
Comes the next season, still he ventures like,

Again repelled ; so to the Westward, now,
He sets his sails, and all the icebergs moots,
And measures them along the floating strand.
Four times his dauntless craft is fitted out,
And now he threads that bay whose cognomen
Is his, which stretches to the warmer South,
Into the half-productive temperature,
If not full grained, and where the woods begin.
Some hundred miles he peers into the West ;
Then wears the winter on some outlet isle,
The harpy winter, fiercest of the climes.
But, ah ! what cruel haps upbraid him, while
The spring looks brighter from the distant noon !
Storms and starvation hold an equal share
In their discomfiture, who there had cast
Their anchor, hoping for the coming sun ;
Those drive them random-dashed. this makes them gaunt.
They grow to mutiny, and turn against
Their moveless captain, stoic to their whims ;
So maddened faithless by their wild distress,
And in their perishing ferocity,
They set him on the ocean's waste adrift,
On a crazed boat alone, while they proceed
A remnant t' England back, but lacking him.
Alas ! none meet him, none he finds ; he fades,
Forever lost in th' all o'erpowering waves !
What verse shall pay his memory all its dues,
What record tune his praise's full desert ;
His persevering traits, his tireless zeal,
And his undaunted front 'mid direst ills,
Unyielding firm, e'en tho', perchance, too stern,
What chord shall twine to all their just degree.
 Here, here's the outlet, here, from Hudson's Bay
To the Pacific, many a one believes,
And some are sanguine, now, they thence shall speed,
Soon wafted, with some slender hindrance sole,
At the first portal o' th' still gentler route,
Thus several expeditions thither crowd

In several years, and make some slight amends
To what discovery antecedent knew,
But find full soon their onward progress barred.
 Hail, Baffin, too, that far away explored
The bay, which speaks of him, and farther North.
How far he penetrated, how exact
His survey was, it needs but to be told,
For half a century none could go beyond
His own far reach, could add a single weight
To his own observation, or could lend
His note of all that was or is, reproof ;
Hail, Baffin, too, that satisfied the best !
 Meanwhile, the Russian would not be outdone,
But thro' the chilled Siberia sought the path,
Now, the Northeast, and only failure met,
Yet not the less persisted many a day.
Now, Behring sailed, whose name the ocean bears,
'Tween Asia and America, the strait.
Hard is their fate that Frost and tempest both
Brave and encounter. Twice the strenuous gales
Drive them, the weather-beaten coast from thence,
Long buffeted before ; and Behring died.
Wrecked were their vessels, then, the wretched crews
An island wintered there, which shelter gave
Such as the sun's drear absence may allow;
And when the Spring looked up, a lesser barque
They built them there, and sailed in dubious plight,
And to Kamschatka reached whence they had sped,
That season's annual anniversary, last.
 Let not unmentioned Shalaroff be passed,
That later went, and perished with his host,
For lack of food for which they could not cruise ;
Nor Andrejeff, nor Billings. Others went,
Still others, who no farther note demand,
Till yet another century had expired,
When Wrengel, Anjou, on trim sledges drove
Right to'ard the North, but found at last the flood,
And were arrested, thus, in forward march.

So well convinced does Russia since refrain
The Polar exploration to disturb,
Since little grew from all her efforts made,
And she perceives, when navies are unfurled
The ice impedes, when swifter sledges drive,
The open seas emerge and bid them halt,
So much commixed in soft and solid moods,
The fickle element, the ships are pent
And hurled by turns, the rapid cars are stopped,
Or carried where they ne'er themselves would go,
On moving platforms severed from their source.
Thus Russia rests from all that travail there,
And deems the Pole approachless from that zone,
A weary desolation vast and wide,
Should none assume to thwart or seek t' invade.

Or here, or yonder, whether 'twere the track,
Would lend the bold emprize the best reward,
Naught yet Brittania 'll yield the hardy search,
And with Columbia henceforth shares the pride,
To press yet farther to the vast unknown,
Approximate, at least, if never found.

Hearne, Cook and Phipps preceded on the stage
Of new designs, which gave their wiry toils
To science, should they be to traffic lost.
One by Spitzbergen sails, by Behring one,
One o'er land goes, and thrice his course repeats ;
But all are hemmed. The Coppermine, that stream,
Which empties where the frigid horror's worst,
Is traced along its bleak and frozen length.

But now Mackenzie finds a vaster flood,
Called by his name, and threads it from its source ;
Enough—he tracks, and with that meed he rests.

Now Ross and Parry take their twin command ;
Sir Franklin and Buchan the like conjoined,
When years have made advance, on routes diverse,
Those to the West, these to the very North,
So far, their shattered hulks abandon they,
And in two yet remaining reach their homes.

The former find them 'mid the devious sounds
On fresher tracts departed, none had trod
Before, or neared, yet where the native dwelt.
What doubts possess them if the view beyond
Is firm-set ice or land, for all is blank,
Blank, white and moveless. Now the pride they feel
Of true discoveries ; but a tempest threats,
And round they veer, and spend awhile their force
Of exploration still on previous bounds,
Till they return on homeward voyage bent.
   Delayed but not discouraged, Parry is.
Another time he sails with hundred men
Accompanied, and Liddon was his mate ;
The Hecla and the Griper are the ships.
By Barrow's straits they rapid ran, and passed,
How many divers islands, headlands, bays.
How near confusion 'mid the tortuous round,
Awaits them, but they press undeviate on,
How oft beleagured by the gelid mass,
Now sweeping ruinous or embedding fast,
Ev'n to Prince Regent's inlet, farther now
Than ever they had gone, than mariner yet
Had touched before them, far compare beyond,
To the magnetic pole approach they, where
The needle 's naught, and neither turns or points.
   Would they yet solve the problem, would they find
The Northwest passage? How their bosoms beat
With fond anticipations, high resolve !
Forward, o'ercoming various obstacles,
Or shunning them, with fresher courage nerved,
They push, as if they were than men ev'n more,
And had 'yond mortals, now, a tenuous will ;
A host of ills and fresh impediments,
With which to cope would none have heart or faith
In common moods, they grapple with, encheered.
But now the frozen hoards enclose them swift,
And they are stopped supreme. They cut their way
Out thro' the solid waters, and return ;

Alas! they must, to Melville isle repaired.
There they invite the winter, and to spend
Prepare, and his phenomena observe,
Tho' terror-built in quiet half repose!
  It was no slight reward for them to cull,
The while, yet less severe the season swayed,
The mosses on the island's western side,
A willow dwarfed, small grass, and saxiprage.
Nor were these matters trivial, which had been
The like before, in their immured retreat,
Since their progressive moments ceased a time;
For knowledge claimed them in such intervals.
When summer, such as is short summer there,
Now lumined, they broke up and floated free,
But soon again were fettered, ere they made
Advance, such as were worthy of the name;
And so forewarned, their purpose they reversed.
Since but a week the mildness may be fled,
And all th' expanse be fixed to bind them fast
Without escape, another long, long year;
So swiftly may the winter warp anew.
They set their face to Britain, hasting thence,
The threatening meshes from, and safe arrive.
  So fortunate a result stirred the mind
Of all Brittania. Parry speeds again.
The Hecla and the Fury wait command.
Long was his cruise, determined was the search.
But little could they add to what the last
Had been achieved. Such endless winter now,
Such blasts unprecedented and ribbed ice,
The most unflagging efforts half are vain,
The weather buffets them from all their aims,
And inauspicious still the more they stay,
They hasten from th' impenetrable clue,
And, therefore, seek the clime from whence they came.
  Could any have made inroads on the pole,
And found fresh knowledge to reward their pains,
Sir Franklin and his six companions sent,

Had been so favored. While the former band
Made their resolved incursion, these, these, too,
Re-entered far th' invulnerable waste,
And many thousand miles they coursed, on foot,
In transient-built canoes, howe'er they could,
Thro' deserts unimaginable, and bare
Of all, save that one element so vast,
That never stint its presence age to age,
Whence e'n the animals had fled away,
The inveterate ruin, once inhabited,
By such a few, but now reduced to none,
And left them famine only, naught of life.
Such steady suffering would none believe,
That man's endurance evermore could brave;
Thus some of them were lost, and some returned,
But failed their full design, their prime desire,
So to co-operate with them that went
On ships, succeeding, on the distant road.
 Great is the prize, and England will not halt.
A four-fold expedition weighs the wave.
First Parry comes, but less successful now,
Than at the first, amid th' ice breaker's wrecked,
And leaves the intolerant wild in one of two,
His chosen vessels which before he sailed.
And Lyon too misfortune only hails,
And wrecked is he ev'n at the portal's edge;
He leaves his transport to the Arctic spoil.
There Beechy harbors in the frozen East,
Sped by Cape Horn t' invade the rigid realm,
And penetrates thro' Behring's strait, unmarred,
To Kotzebue's far Sound, on the Ocean's brink.
There waits Sir Franklin, overland, the last
Of the four venturous parties. On the snow,
The ice, the rivers, or th' ice-blocking sea,
He fares undaunted. Beechy waits, again,
Where he departed late while danger loomed,
When the next year gives promise to success.
In vain he waits. Sir Franklin shall not reach

That rendezvous, tho' now full sure within
But half an hundred leagues, are each from each,
Unknown to them, so near ; they never met.
Thus all the fleet their solitary way
Took, broken or dispersed, the parties all.
What had they met they had not earlier known?
That great first problem was so much at heart,
No nearer to solution than at first,
But knowledge still they gathered naught remiss.
Whate'er the earth or flood afforded, yet,
Whatever Nature offered to the view,
Or latent hoarded, mysteries in their bud,
Terrestrial wonders and celestial sights,
And secret influences were only there,
In native cogency, they marked and culled ;
Their hopes, tho' empty that Northwest to find,
Their aim, so constant, still, yet not in vain.
 If any should have precedence, where all,
Or where so many are devoted well,
Then that distinction, Parry, should be thine,
That with heroic fortitude pursued
Thy stern vocation, happiest in its maze.
A veteran, the more he fain persists,
And now with new device the Pole attacks.
The boat and sledge conjoined, fresh trust inspires.
The crews advance—alas ! the faithless hoards
Betray their footing ; faster as they speed,
The faster fleet the ice-fields to the south,
And many days they forward go, but back,
Full oft' as far involuntary borne
By the receding float, they retrograde,
Ev'n when they're swiftest in their forward step ;
And that which shed best auguries proves them null.
Next Ross sailed in Victoria ship, prepared
For storm and calm by steam and canvass both.
He found the magnet's centre, farther on
Than any still, he measured recent coasts,
And 'mid the multitudinous inlets strayed.

What dire events, what most terrific gales,
What scarce less horrent calms they dwell amid;
What loathe disease, the baleful scurvy, kills—
These need no speech, the wont alternative
Of them that probe the desolation weird,
The Arctic amplitude alive t' invest.
  And others still make to th' incognito,
Back, Roe, and else th' enthusiasts for the quest,
And find new lands, and add to distances;
And now behold th' explorers, sanguine-eyed,
Ev'n to a narrow compass th' inlets proved,
Narrow, compared to all they've hither passed,
What isles, what headlands, what innumerous nooks,
What deviate bays, what smooth expanses far,
As well as rugged-riv'n, could no one tell,
So icy-mantled still, was 't land or flood.
Yet, not for them to pass that boundary's depth,
Or know its texture; still there still is much
To fitly scan and hard to ascertain.
  Plead they another's cause, what daring chief
Was e'er more chivalrous than Franklin, thou?
Again he sails, a well-appointed crew,
A hardy band, an hundred and a score
Their numbers are. Upon its axle twice
The year hath turned, no word from him arrives,
And in his country's bosom fears arise,
That in those awful deeps he may be lost,
Or bear privation which he cannot ward.
So to his rescue many a seaman hastes,
To mention all were but a waste of time.
But not a trace th' investigators find,
Till five long seasons round, defeated still;
Then, Ommancy, of the Assistance, meets, at last,
Such relics of Cape Riley as give proof
The so long sought for once had there delayed:
A house embankment, and the site of tents
Were paved with stones, and vacant lodges round
With empty canisters, or else, and last to note,

Three graves which bore the winter's early date,
But naught a record told where were they, now,
Or whither went they thence? How many sought
T' elucidate the question naught avails ;
From Britain, from the Union of the States,
Whence, too, De Haven sped in earnest aid,
From east to west, t' approach the doubt unsolved.
Thrice Lady Franklin fits her convoys out,
And thrice in vain, she mourns her widowed hopes.
Twelve vessels were they entered at the east
For information, naught their fate reveals,
Who went so courageous, so long ago,
Naught till five years again, their term approach.
Rae meets the natives who their plunder bear,
And the Esquimaux point where their corpses lie,
And some have tombs upon the continent.
There is the bitter frost the most extreme,
By William's land and where Back river's frost.
Rae goes, and others go, and find the like,
The vestiges of all the ruin round,
With names of ships and men on billets carved ;
The remnant here'd succumbed, and chilled to death,
Six years upon the miserable expanse !
What praise shall now revive thee, what laments
Shall wail the fit, the hero of the North,
Ennobled by thy martyrdom, thy toils ?
Who shall but emulate thy stern delights?
It was thine iron joy surpassing joys,
Upon the glittering barrenness to be
A large existence mid the lone extent,
The biting deathliness and pallid glare ;
The Arctic was thy home ; as well as thy grave,
And there thou pausest by th' eternal snow ;
The everlasting barriers find thee room.
Ah, me ? is it worth all the tedious while,
To pay such prices for the means to know ?
Boots it to them, that e'en the north exists,
Or not, so much, who have full much to do,

To keep their souls from mildew where they are?
There wave the gales still desolate, as when
They first were stiffened; there th' encumbered sail
Hath no fruition yet, and e'er will be
Thus unproductive, tho' ten thousand roved
The circuit daily. Nay—is not of th' earth
Mankind the lord? Their planets, record should
They not hold legible; with knowledge grows
Man, growing too, and is the more th' earth's lord,
What Heav'n designed him when created, there?
Meantime not idly did th' explorers wait,
And Belcher, Inglefield were foremost, now.
Five ships were Belchers, two, proud steamers, hailed.
How fortunate was he would none dispute
Whom glad Benevolence so well could land.
He met McClure and rescued him, three years,
Buried three long long years in the Arctic ice,
And well nigh spent; yes he was prosperous, too.
He pierced the deep remote, the confine saw,
And near the terminus from sea to sea,
Of Barrows strait, the North-West passage found,
Thereafter proved by them before they part.
They leave their fleet, abandoned, more than half
Behind, and speed in three ships to England's shore.
   Oh! for a signal beam to celebrate
The conquered barrier! Yet, what barque will glide
There through, mid the ceaseless ice, so far,
The cont'nent to the isles conjointed yond,
As tho' twere still the land, and not the strait,
The entrance shining! None. And still it waits
In loneliness, intangible, unshorn,
Wrapped in cold dreams, as first, and Science wins,
Alone, what Navigation ne'er can gain.
Last Kane departs, sped from Columbian ports,
And gives his youth in th' Arctic peril spent
The sequel's phase, he windeth up the thread
Of that intelligence the Pole that braved,
Which would not yield his countenance to him,

Three graves which bore the winter's early date,
But naught a record told where were they, now,
Or whither went they thence? How many sought
T' elucidate the question naught avails ;
From Britain, from the Union of the States,
Whence, too, De Haven sped in earnest aid,
From east to west, t' approach the doubt unsolved.
Thrice Lady Franklin fits her convoys out,
And thrice in vain, she mourns her widowed hopes.
Twelve vessels were they entered at the east
For information, naught their fate reveals,
Who went so courageous, so long ago,
Naught till five years again, their term approach.
Rae meets the natives who their plunder bear,
And the Esquimaux point where their corpses lie,
And some have tombs upon the continent.
There is the bitter frost the most extreme,
By William's land and where Back river's frost.
Rae goes, and others go, and find the like,
The vestiges of all the ruin round,
With names of ships and men on billets carved ;
The remnant here'd succumbed, and chilled to death,
Six years upon the miserable expanse !
What praise shall now revive thee, what laments
Shall wail the fit, the hero of the North,
Ennobled by thy martyrdom, thy toils ?
Who shall but emulate thy stern delights ?
It was thine iron joy surpassing joys,
Upon the glittering barrenness to be
A large existence mid the lone extent,
The biting deathliness and pallid glare ;
The Arctic was thy home ; as well as thy grave,
And there thou pausest by th' eternal snow ;
The everlasting barriers find thee room.
Ah, me? is it worth all the tedious while,
To pay such prices for the means to know ?
Boots it to them, that e'en the north exists,
Or not, so much, who have full much to do,

To keep their souls from mildew where they are?
There wave the gales still desolate, as when
They first were stiffened ; there th' encumbered sail
Hath no fruitian yet, and e'er will be
Thus unproductive, tho' ten thousand roved
The circuit daily. Nay—is not of th' earth
Mankind the lord? Their planets, record should
They not hold legible ; with knowledge grows
Man, growing too, and is the more th' earth's lord,
What Heav'n designed him when created, there ?
Meantime not idly did th' explorers wait,
And Belcher, Inglefield were foremost, now.
Five ships were Belchers, two, proud steamers, hailed.
How fortunate was he would none dispute
Whom glad Benevolence so well could land.
He met McClure and rescued him, three years,
Buried three long long years in the Arctic ice,
And well nigh spent ; yes he was prosperous, too.
He pierced the deep remote, the confine saw,
And near the terminus from sea to sea,
Of Barrows strait, the North-West passage found,
Thereafter proved by them before they part.
They leave their fleet, abandoned, more than half
Behind, and speed in three ships to England's shore.
  Oh ! for a signal beam to celebrate
The conquered barrier ! Yet, what barque will glide
There through, mid the ceaseless ice, so far,
The cont'nent to the isles conjointed yond,
As tho' twere still the land, and not the strait,
The entrance shining ! None. And still it waits
In loneliness, intangible, unshorn,
Wrapped in cold dreams, as first, and Science wins,
Alone, what Navigation ne'er can gain.
Last Kane departs, sped from Columbian ports,
And gives his youth in th' Arctic peril spent
The sequel's phase, he windeth up the thread
Of that intelligence the Pole that braved,
Which would not yield his countenance to him,

More than the rest, tho' nearer to his glance
He pried than all, and of his occult smile
One sole flash apprehended, following none
Nor anteceding, inaccessive else.
There he remains with that disabled far
The beckoning prize, yet to elude him still,
And vanished now, he flies t' the soothing South,
In the West Indies breathes the balmy clime;
There yields existence to the malady,
Caught from the Boreal shaft too deep to heal.
What farther, later, yet befalls, is veiled
In deep obscurity; the history's closed.

BOOK II.

THE VOYAGE.

Amid the ice-bergs—what a host of them?
Like shining citadels, a front some part
Upon the sea: like stony monuments
And sculptured tombs, or islets, worn
To polished rocks by liquidating waves!
Fleet had they sped, their never wearying sail
The Night and Terror named. None were they here,
Mid th' outworks of the Arctic haply thralled,
Nay, not so long the tempest did not wake
To its full anger, or the mists too deep,,
And total darkness bade their vision fail,
Were they so wrecked; for peaceful are the bergs,
And give them room, and still their latitude.
By yonder crystal mass they anchor, now;
How slowly on it moves, or stillness seems

To guard it from its just mobility?
Or is it fixed, and does not seem to stay,
Most truly, and defeats its journey South?
They moor their vessel to it; now, they climb
The slippery side with ladders set—ah! too
Precipitous for safety, yet but leave
Them plenteous minutes they will make full sure,
By speedy matches chiselled in the rime!
And thus they do ascend, and on the top
Of lucid turrets, by sharp pinnacles,
Stand and survey the all embracing floods
From heights serene, none else around such heights.
 Prone to diversion for a moment, thus
They play indulge ; but soon their purpose calls,
And they unloose themselves th' uncertain hold.
They speed auspicious, for the gales are set
In tides propulsive ; yet, 'tis perilous still,
For should some floating breaker, yet as strong
As 'twere firm founded, 'scape their constant note,
So oft full half immersed, the while the storm
Rose boisterous higher, ere they deemed as much,
No mighty marvel 'twere if they were doomed.
Therefore they keep their vigilance alert,
Scarce less than when more imminent danger dares ;
Tho' danger 's always some sort on the brine,
Since this is added :—steer, and keep th' eye bright.
 Such was the recreant fate so late befell
The noble Arctic, armed by mighty steam,
Caught in th' o'er-passing fogs of Newfoundland,
Are bred by Labrador, far out the shore,
Th' encountering iceberg met, she straight went down
With all on board, a thousand numbering near.
None ever heard of them, or saw a trace
Of her wrecked frame, the ocean's total spoil,
Since e'er that kate. What else in that mid sea
Could e'er have made such perfect havoc but
These annual scavengers, this awe of the deep?
 Why were these monsters given to the wave?

Is not the salt sea wider than the land?
There they disport the most enormous whales;
Like hidden ledges they obscure the foam ;
Like wavy fountains, here and there they spout ;
Like geysers which in Iceland violent break
In fragments, yet more natural, they fleck
Their populous abodes, these mammoth tribes.
   Hail to the whalers! see, they, too, are there !
Now these adventurers observe the chase.
The ship is distant, but the boatmen come
Yet nearer, and these meet their half advance.
There did they first harpoon the creature huge,
Significant, not fatal, where he rose
To blow his breath, that all the sea disturbs
And shakes around him. No, he does not die ;
Yet in a soft and vital part they struck.
He flies ; they follow swift as hands can row
By six stout oarsmen wielded, while the line
Bales out more swiftly still. But first they made,
When they had wounded th' animal so large,
A sign immediate—th' oars turned into poles,
Upright and visible. The watchman sees
From the still ship, and cries a loud alarm.
The ready boats do hear, and start at once
To rescue or to aid. They come, they come !
Are with them now. whose rope is well nigh run,
And fasten this to you, a doubled length.
Now the chase rises up, for he must breathe,
And spouts again. He loiters, by his wound
Enfeebled haply, for his crimson blood
The frequent jets do tinge, and seeks to soothe
His novel pangs, his large anxieties,
His most unwonted toils, such never known
Within the lambent sun or cooler surge,
And float at ease more purely in th' ether fanned.
Thus they arrive who sedulous pursued,
And nearer, strike again. He flies once more,
Now maddened, and the clue still multiplied

Unwinds precipitant. But he must halt,
And rise to breathe again before 'tis spent,
The keeping, holding cord ; and now he pines,
Too much exhausted by exerted strength
So late employed, and efforts fraught with fear,
Mysterious wrought. So when they find him there,
Near passive is he. Oft they strike ; he moves,
But not to dip, or slide away, and down ;
He seeks the more the balmy atmosphere,
The ventilating breeze, and more repose.
They drag him now, all helpless he, and pierce
Him to the death indubitable found,
The vast levathan a lamb as tame,
And tow him to the ship. There, iron-heeled,
They mount the carcass, and cut joyful thence
The heavy slabs of blubber, oil and bone,
They render up and haul upon the deck,
Then leave the skeleton float, a worthless prey.

 Another scene. There, at the second stroke
Of th' instrument drawn at the second rise,
The vast sea monster lashs his awful tail,
So suddenly, and so stupendous wrought,
The waters roar like rushing thunder heard.
The hapless crew, too eager for the prize,
Await too near, or cannot speed so soon,
And with one blow are shivered into shreds
The boat and all. He plunges to the deeps,
And dives immense, but th' other floats assume
The lost one's place ; ascends he, now, again.
They're fearless by, and soon transfix him, o'er
And o'er repeat the gushing lances ; now he's weak,
He is so weak, and soon he yields, a wreck
Of life, an episode for the harm he did.

 Yet others run so fast, th' augmented lines
Are soon exhausted ere they all are joined,
Or when they are they cannot follow swift
Enough to keep within the lengthened bound.
The fleeting whale draws them and dashes them

Adown the billows, so regardless he
The jarring pains that rive him. They must cut
The long continuous cord, or quickly sink,
The victims of temerity and delay,—
And leave him loose, perchance, they'll meet once more.
  These hardy and unshrinking mariners,
Hence from Nantucket, or the recent West,
Or Brighton, or Brittania, hailing oft,
The unicorn of th' ocean spear, profuse,
The narwhal take, whate'er the game affords,
Whalebone and spermaceti, venturous prize,
For commerce gained and th' arts, to furnish man's
Proud luxuries with choicer ministries.
Untiring, stern pursuit, such frost, and toils
Which scarce have parallel, they welcome brave,
And enter keener than the battle's rank
The martial hosts, the wild and watery sports,
Far from companionship remote, amid
The loneliness, th' immeasurable expanse,
Monotonous, save them who pauseless seek
The lively conflict, coveted, as a wreath
Of victory their briny brows to crown;—
Till these cetaceous races disappear,
Full half-from all the varied, vast marine,
Which here or there these mighty mammals know
No more, extinct, or flown to other floods.
  Speed on, brave barque. The pilgrims onward hie,
And leave these later prospects dimmed behind,
By prosperous breezes wafted far beyond.
Now glows the night with less than temperate gloom,
But by the lunar beam illumed, yet,
And far the vessel's wake the track expands,
Like to the scintillations of the stars,
Like to the splendors of the milky way,
Till fading far aback the endless view.
  Blest are the eyes that Greenland first behold,
The rocky rampart of the Polar Zone,
The prop impregnable of th' icy weight:

Blest are those eyes when for the Pole alive,
And anxious to survive, are for the Pole,
Where Boreas dwells, and sheds his frosty blight
O'er half the lands, when winter makes approach ;
Yet oft is benison and strews it too,
Where tepid waves are putrid still, and dull
The stagnant airs, and febrile pulses beat :
He purifies and cools the torrid blare,
And nerves again the invigorate atmosphere,
Late paralized, and braces feeble man,
By his incongruous storms and rugged phase,
Now mild and mellowed in their distant reach ;
Or only when the sun the year descends,
He curbs and flagellates the Temperate Zone,
But yet is health and summer bountiful ;
But here, within his native region throned,
Is ever tyranous from moon to moon.

   Greenland they greet, that rough and sturdy belt,
That binds the North by Denmark colonized.
Lyman, the sage commander, Theobald,
The naturalist, Alphonse, th' architect,
Moulton, the astronomer, and Christiansen,
The Esquimaux youth, whom they at Fiskerneas
Engaged, grown up so docile, he would serve
Them much the natives 'mid, their fare to find,
With hunt successful on the land or flood,—
With Gerrit, secretary, were the chief
O' th' venturous band, whom fifteen pilgrims else
Accompanied, and cheerful duty gave,
And well abettors were in all their plight.
With twice a score select of canine brood,
They added to the store they brought away,
From Newfoundland, of that uncommon race,
They leave the brotherhood of man once more,
Except themselves, and bid farewell the past,
Not without sanguine hopefulness, and glad,
To meet such novelties, and fresh delights
E'en tho' unmingled with a hue severe.

Once more among the icebergs, how they float,
But adverse to the drift that seeks the noon,
The midnight they? The floes would drive them back,
The lodges and the platitudes of ice;
And oft they anchor themselves to a rock
Of solid element, and thence are rowed
Insensibly 'gainst surface and the wind.
This now beats higher, oft they separate,
Driv'n half at random, or another seek
To overtake of these more firm-set hosts,
Capricious less, nor subject to the breeze,
And bid it lead them forth, and give them speed.
But now they drive, urged by the harsher storm
And traverse wave, loosed from their anchor long,
Upon a slope of ice, unconscious they,
That far subtends the surface, underneath
Deep hidden, more and more they rise; at once
They do perceive; too late,—they cannot move
Th' untimely bulk, even to the frowning top
They go apparent, and each moment fear
Their overthrow, the vessel sideling cast.
  Erect she stays, and ne'ertheless maintains
Her balanced figure. Gracious fate prolongs
Their still security, she grinds along
The ridges cleft, a not unfit ravine
Imbeds her there, and now she halts, propelled
No longer from without by wind and tide,
Upon an iceberg. Long they ponder not,
But quick depart the frame, and scan her hold.
  Some stray upon the rimy rafts without;
For now th' aerial current calms, but all
Flee from the darkened shadow of the hulk.
Tho' yet it wavers not, who knows how soon
'Twill settle sinister and overhaul,
And dip destruction 'mid the shattering brinks.
Let them rejoice again—at last she slides,
The mountain moves away; by th' icy blocks
No more beleaguered backward, nor the breeze,

She drops relieved, and swims as bouyantly
And native as tho' upon the solid flood
She ne'er had stranded. They assume the deck,
And take their course, nor ship or crew the worse.
  Escape so imminent how oft is theirs!
Now 'mid the partial night they forward bilge,
Cast from their berths who sleep, but right again,
In great degree, by shelves and props sustained
Of broken masses now, that give them free.
Now by the drift enclosed they labor through,
But cannot long, and now must cut their way
By axe and edge. Now 'tween two glaciers caught,
Which threat to meet and crush them in their folds,
Just when they emerge, they leave them to the shock,
That gnashes its teeth. Now in the driving mesh
Of ice redoubled planes they fear to fall,
So thrust and piled, they well may break their sides,
E'en the next moment; still the snare they escape,
And find an opening where they had not weened.
Now by a boulder on a single stem
Aloft expanded fan-like to the height,
Like high arcades and eaves on every side,
Beneath whose shelter ships may roomy ride,
They pass unprovided. They burst afront
In splintered ribs, and fall away in drops,
Pierced by the ceaseless sun, like shooting hail,
And startle like near musketry the width:
Then to the icy shore are pressed too close,
Too nearly riven where the bolts impinge
A minute, but go by and liberate
The groaning craft, e'en ere their hope expects.
  Thus day by day th' interminable waste
Inclines afar. Now from the verging bay
They pass the pondrous gates, the rocking sills,
And to the strait make entrance. There they pause,
And lend their voyage forth a breathing spell
At Refuge Harbor. Now their ravenous dogs
Demand such sustenance they cannot spare,

And out upon the void the sailors throng
For the hunt eager. Lo! the walrus meets
The apt commander, and he pierces him!
A deadly shaft he feels, and dies forthwith.
They bring him inward drawn, a massive weight,
A slender feast for all the hungry pack,
But temporary, tho' so great a bulk.
   The sea-horse is the northern elephant;
In rolling droves like herding swine he haunts
The landed tracts, but must invoke the sea
For provender. Where would he find his food
Amid that utter barenness if not
Within the deeps? His tusk is like
His prototype's, more precious yet; he lives
In flood, on field; he battles for his young,
Firm as the eagles in their higher homes,
But yet is sluggish, for the waves may hide
Him quickly; there his prey he meets unsought;
His fat is like the huge balaenae's, too,
A less proportion, yet a teeming weight.
   Advance they now. Horror on horror greets
Them more than want. Herculean toils engage
Them every step, and cares untaught afflict.
The ices drive them back, they thro' them bore.
The roseate cliffs in distant view adorn
The deep horizon now; the crimson snow
Is like the frame of tapestry beyond,
Soft woven, close, and like the purple star,
Beyond the zenith beaming sweeter dyes.
   How far shall they go forth? When shall they stop?
Will they not thence be hemmed beyond release?
Will they make headway yet, or shall they yield?
The ominous ice blink threatens; see, above
The dull reflection. There the gelid fields,
Impenetrable, would arrest their march,
This phase declares, if sooner not, 'tis stemmed.
Here the thick ledges cumulate, enforced,
And harbinger the plight at distance sure

If not already their impediments
Be too potential ev'n to dare that sign,
And curb them here encompassed, shut, and fixed
Immovable, or shattered into shreds,
Ev'n here, before they reach that farther belt.
   Return is not for them, but safe they seek
An inner bight, and rest them, to survey
The looming probabilities a-while,
Ere farther venture make they. Yet they try
A next endeavor, timely, but in vain ;
They find the masses closer, deeper pent,
The barrier wider. Thus they do retrace
Their exit speedy, and adopt the cove,
Their rescue, and good harbor mid the drift.
   For now the partial summer gins to wane,
The short-lived season, and the drearier winds
Begin to rave. The long continuous orb
Of day moves lower, now, and more averse,
Whose midnight sunshine casts a drizzly ray,
A light that's like a melancholy dirge,
Disastrous fading far along the scope ;
And for a spell he sinks oblivious now,
Where but the luminous twilight points his place.
Alas ! for them who there may dwell immured,
When he departs, when he departs and comes
No more, from hour to many a weary hour?
Save that they bury them within the earth
In dusky canes, 'tis horrible, and them,
'Tis truly gloom undoubted there to dwell :
But ships may be made frost proof, they within
Should they ne'er venture out, or need go forth,
The while th' incontinent, cold rigors reign.
   Is there no sapient prospect to prevail,
And farther penetrate the hostile bourne ?
They husbanded the hours ; but who shall helm
The downward torrent and propulsive rafts
Against full speeded ? Thus their slow advance
Is yet intent, and still additional,

Whatever bars, thro' most the double days.
But for the present they must patient wait.
They go t' explore the near contingency, and far,
The indications, while their latitude
Is farther forth than cruise there ever went.
  A part stay with the rescued brig, the rest
Proceed with sledges north along the coast,
Embatted still by walls a thousand feet,
And oftime higher still by beetling rocks;
But here and there a deep ravine extends,
And plains diverge. Around the jutting shore,
A crystal esplanade engirds the heights,
A parapet solidified, as pure
As gems of the first water, and as fair
As th' ether when no mist the day invests.
'Tis their they search, except they deviate
In their excursion to the inland bent.
  What have they now? They halt a space surprised.
The ruined huts of former natives these,
And yet so ruinous, they know them scarce
To specify from those surrounding blocks
Of stone, transported thence from farther parts,
Save by inspection nearer. What are these?
Their implements,—their toys, their hooks, their spears.
And here are graves, a dome of pebbles piled,
A cairn above; upon their haunches rest
The skeletons, and ever there repose:
They by their kindred ne'er will be disturbed;
They hold their relics sacred as their lives.
" Deserted huts! perchance the blast to serve
Was here for them, ev'n them, the wintry scourge,
Who habited, yet we come far t' abide
The season's utmost frown," Alphonse exclaims.
Whom Lyman answers thus: "They need but roam;
They have it else, and they know more than we,
Much as they need to know, and most of this:
We need the aliment the world affords
To feed the flame of knowledge and of love,

Ulterior objects give us argument."
  Farther they go. A glacier fronts their path,
They wish to climb, so far it juts beyond
Their course direct. The slippery side they mount
With toil and danger, yet secure ascend
And downward drop. Beneath the darksome shade
Of frowning cliffs they wander, now amazed.
Magnesia, lime and sandstone grit are made
Their element, and greenstone boulders mar
The steepy slopes from distant borders borne.
Here only by the overhanging mould,
Or height precipitous the rocks are bare,
Or where the nooks are sunward, or the rime
In furrowed channels runs, a melted maze!
  Lo! the sea swallows from their eyric perched,
The latest flock before their eyes depart,
The last of all the plumy tribes to leave
The scowling scope, prophetic of the gloom,
Which soon befalls, the scatheless snow-bird sole
Remains content, when all the rest have fled;
The gentle spirit of the filmy storm,
He revels there; his pleasure is the snow.
Here are there musk-ox remnants; ages since
He roamed these regions; now his milken coat,
As soft, as white, as whitest wool, he doffs
Within these sterile bounds no more; his range
Is westernmost, and 'yond this sea he lives,
A beacon of the perished past these bones.
  A snow-fall! see, the sky o'erclouds! How mild,
How gentle, with the clattering ice compared,
The flaky showers! And, yet, 'tis loneliness
More sensible than by the crashing spars.
A dimmer void, they seem shut out from all
The living, now, tho' yet in truth they'd naught
Companionship before, than now more full;
The harsh resounding resonance is hushed,
And leaves them pondering with their absent thoughts.
  Beyond a file of headlands crosses them;

They overcome them wh'le the welkin clears.
Retarded still and clogged by all the load
They bear along, a depot they provide,
And build a cairn; with native colors fixed,
A firm-set-staff. Perchance some traveller here,
Some weary wanderer well nigh undone,
May the memento find in future hours,
And feel fresh energy his heart t' inspire.
Or they, themselves, may in their devious course
Be thereby guided yet, and sometime meet
Well-timed provisions there, their former track,
Pre-occupied and sustenant, thence to cull
A bracing consolation mid their wants.
   Forsooth, there's a marvel. Here a river rolls
And roars tumultuous, o'er its rocky bed,
And wide as a large city's streets are long,
By inward glaciers fed, majestic hoards,
That raise above their massive, glittering piles,
A full day's journey inland, whence the stream
Bears down, impetuous driv'n, and meets the tide
For miles ascending,. Here the Arctic blooms.
The flowers, cruciferous and the poppies lift
Their leaves and petals ; th' andromeda ripes
Amid the affluent mosses, and the rest
Are green and beautiful amid the nooks.
Where'er the summer beats more full, where'r
The sunny rays impinge, and from the rocks
Reverberate, the watery ooze distils,
In warm recesses pent, or sunward turned,
These tender messengers of life spring up,
And clothe the barr'n with quick economy,
And bounty teeming, as in added haste,
T' improve the genial hours so fleeting flown,—
With quicker diligence, than where of time
They've lengthened lease to grow, and plenteous room :
And therefore deck the bound surprisingly,
In crevices beside the neighboring frost.
   Now on the last bold height the Pilgrims stand ;

They view the Arctic highlands. Fuller than
Before they shine behind them, and exalt
Their varied shapes. Beyond, afar there beams
Of solid ice a sea without a rent,
Indefinite, and vast, as 'twere the earth
Were all congealed, so interminable far,
So universal mid the dazzling light,
But vision rendering, yet a mound there gleams
Still yonder at the vista's terminus,
An ice-built temple on the weary plain,
To check th' unending level. Save the bleak,
Oft perpendicular, bare, riven rock,
Near by, and scarce to note amid the marge
All else is ice, a stagnant wave of ice.
    No more, the goal is found. The friends return
With more facility than first they went,
Save that a hurricane impedes them now ;
But this is less precarious on the land
Than on the antag'nist element, yet they
May lose their hold, and slide upon the brinks ;
They bide the pitiless surge till the angers 's spent.
They hail their fellows these behold them glad,
And query them. The doubt is o'er, they must
Abide the year's stern rigors here resolved.
Five days they had departed ; now they turn
Into their quarters, while the young ice breaks
And forms around in slush : the voyage ends.

BOOK III.

WINTER-QUARTERS.

Unseen the sun will be ere many days;
The night comes on, and sooner than 'twould else,
That orb will be invisible,—a ridge
Expands before their lodge, and shuts him out
A fortnight earlier than he truly sets,
Or never rises at the highest noon.
  But this privation partial's balanced by
Advantage greater. Th' outward-driving ice
Encroaches ne'er, and scarce the storms can reach
Th' interior shelter walled on every side,
Save to the southward when the day mounts high
Admitting him, unmitigate and full,
And earlier melts the frost, and liberates
The ship ev'n sooner than beyond there's room.
  Provision, now, the Pilgrims make, the best
T' inhabit there, and spend the wintry round,
In foresight wakeful for their every need.
Already there the stolid iceberg 's chained,
Imprisoned from his unremitting march;
The separate floes compact and bind their seams,
And soon the element one fast expanse
Will be continuous, frozen and alike.
  The inaccessible, the proud, the vast,
Say, what unwonted pow'r t' attract it hath?
It stirs th' incipient aspiration's sigh;
It tempts the hid ambition to explore;
And ev'n these everlasting solitudes
To penetrate, to bear, to ascertain,
The soul endeavors, and th' abhorrent dares

With cheerfulness not of itself alone.
   Lead me to other bow'rs, let me recline
Where summer ne'er the season quite resigns,
And but a contrast sweet the winter is,
A blest variety, a gentle change,
Tho' harsher, not severe; tho' cold, yet mild,
The sun's monotony to diversify.
There on that ground debate'ble let me stay,
When the four winds hold counsel yet contend,
Shorn of their worst extremes, a medium phase
T' assume congenial with the veins of life,
So modified to all their best intents,
Where the fond birds may sing the round year long,
With leisure, marred not by th' *invigorate* clime,
But not *consuming*, or by fire or frost.
   But there are those disdain the milder paths,
Or choose the sterner, by true nature taught,
Or habit, or strong education's bent,
By pride, by pow'r, by noble virtues fired;
Whose lofty minds are grieved by common things,
And have they choice their circumstance select,
The battle's furor rather than its lull,
Would wrestle with the storm and bid it shrink,
And tempt the elements to yield them note,
And conjure up the might where danger lures.
And have their gladness where there's toil and fear,
Destruction, teeming oft. Th' avenging forms
Ask retribution for th' obtrusive touch,
Their long obscurity would from them wrest,
And all their latent mysteries unveil;
Would tamper with their wont consistency:
Thus th' angered haunt them with relentless wrath.
   Leave them to their deserts; each hath its sphere,
But me the easier temperature invites;
Leave them to their deserts, who thus are prone,
Who thus have theme, condition, aim, and place:
In the world's page they fill a varied blank,
Were never else supplied. They have their meed,

And amplify the world with high command;
Proud honors twine their garlands; be they wreathed
In hues supernal, never more to pale.
  Ho, for the hunt! A chosen party go,
And traps they build the silver fox to pen.
They find the hare, where in his warren he
Is unmolested, save that Reynard track.
They meet the reindeer flocks; their mantle gray
Was once, perchance, in hue a fawn or brown;
But now is like, as all that here abides,
The all encircling, all engrossing hues
Of all the amplitude, both far and near,
A perfect whiteness, scarce a shade's relief.
  Far to th' interior is their frosty raid,
O'er the compacted or the powdery flakes;
And Christiansen points out the likely game,
Where they resort, where aptest are they found,
Innocuous, or encountered unaware.
They feel the frost, but are not prone to freeze;
Their teguments are less disintegrate
By the warmth's absence, than their hot-blood mates'
In blander latitudes; but yet they hide
In sheltered attitudes 'mid slower drifts
Of th' airy current, half their edges dulled.
A week 'mid dry-land glaciers occupied,
And over-capping gorges, and white plains,
And oft indented plateaus, they return,
And meet their comrades with a plenteous spoil;
And since they know full well the herded haunts,
And oftime bring a victim to the fare.
  Some date before thrown outward by the waves,
A narwhal they encounter, dead—but yet
Preservative, and for the canine crowd
A benefaction. Long that huge supply
Will feed them fully. Thus there's divers food,
And meat abundant both for man and beast.
Meantime they yoke their elfin, active teams,
And train them diligent, the docile dogs,

The Newfoundlanders and the Esquimaux,
Till they are learned and know their ready round.
    And now the moving waste is fixed, they start
On that excursion to provide the means
Of future providence. The sledge is spurred,
And merrily the motley host proceed,
The men enwrapped in treble furs, the brutes
Enharnessed slight, and led by wand or whip.
Here, there, they make a cache, and bury deep,
The stored provision, 'fended well by stones
And massive boulders, lest the wanton bear
Despoil it speedily, whose active scent
Is oft precocious, and whose strength is vast
And quick to overthrow the best built cairn,
And disinter the bounty th' earth would hide.
It needs no labor slight the hardened soil
To excavate, or harder ice; it needs
No slight exposure to perform the jaunt
In all its incidents for later wants.
The task is ended; thrice they have built up
A meat deposit, far toward the north,
As far as former penetrated they,
To guide them afterward, and sustenance
Afford them in their coming far research,
Which they could carry with them ne'er such weight;
For they've a future eye toward the Pole.
    Now turn they back, a long, long ride or walk,
Amid the still augmenting wintryness:
The charioteer looks up, his lash resounds,
The jovial pack dash forward, howling wild.
    How long do they detain! Do they succumb
To the devouring elements a prey,
Or lost their course? Or elsewise can they not
Accomplish their completed purposes?
They have been absent well-nigh thrice a week.
    Lyman departs to seek them or to aid,
With twain assistants. Now they meet
The lagging train, exhausted near, too soon.

"Oh! here you are! Ah! at last have you come?
We feared you'd fail, and would leave us, alone,
To the sharp mercies of the biting blast,
Alone to buffet all this wierd, wan air,
And threatening languor would our steps impede."
    Thus they that yet have voice. "Let us rouse up,
Be cheered," cries Lyman, then. 'Tis willing heed;
They stir them to fresh efforts. Now they march
Encouraging; it is no time to halt.
A snow show'r now encumbers them, and all
The scene invests. So much perforce waylaid,
Upon the soft and pillowy snow now would
They sink and languish dreamily, awhile.
Yet better counsels sway; they shake them from
The drowsy hoards, and their thick blank'ts up fold,
Around them still. At last they come, at last
They hail the brig, at last they enter,—all,
All mad, all muttering wild that yet have tongue,
By the too grand persistence overwrought.
    Yet temporary is that dread effect,
Nor owns a vital tension. They grow sane
Ere long; the mind recovers all its tone.
The cold, more lasting, harms; some member lose
Near all that were so long upon the road,
Fourfold sev'n days well nigh ere they returned.
Ear, finger, foot, or facial feature blanched,
The most complain, and one his pedal limb,
That, hard alternative, and most so there,
Quick amputation only aids to heal.
    What farther from the needful march results?
Otis, the hunter, dies. Too deep the frost
His innermost has touched. Some days he wanes,
Then bids farewell. Seven days, in polar state,
On the forecastle he reposes, they
Then by th' observatory they bury him,
His messmates, where they designate the stars.
    Oft did he find the deer, the hare, and bring
Them down when others could not, or he caught

A fox where others had not weened as much one nigh.
Now, his unbroken vigil is at end.
Nor did the animal race resist the blight ;
Two foreign cubs, tho' still the natives stood,
Did drop away, killed by that drive beyond.
   Who would indwell in such a dread domain,
Save that he were by some great purpose fired ?
Lyman and his companions brave the worst,
The earth's distemperature, ev'n life itself
To forfeit, haply, while the indolent merge
Into pleased lethergy ; they pass it by
The fit occasion slighted, unimproved ;
But these will have reward, an added gift,
To grace their lives with well earned glories yet.
   Comes on the night ; that long privation glooms.
But tho' 'tis darkness, 'tis not dark, but dim,
So indistinct as tho' 'twere all one thing,
As 'tis one hue. The endless twilight 'lumes
The starry circumflex, but yet dispels
The great nocturnal lamps, save thou'd conceive
The moon to brighten from the southern bound,
And flood the vista with prolific rays.
A blaze of radiancy expands, a sea
Of jewelry irradiates the scope ;
Twinkling stalactites and sparkling spars,.
Suspended from the galleries, the halls
Are countless in sweet lustre, and so deep
Their brilliancy, so pure, they pierce the soul:
The streets, the promenades are silver-paved,
But, oh how solitary ! oh, how cold !
In corruscations, infinite and far.
Did the sharp season not forbid one gaze
From some out promitory on all the view,
That vast enchantment ! But a single glance
'Twould sole permit ; the eye must close, or rush
To action all the limbs, and haste away.
Thou canst not gather all the traits, and wait,
And still revolve the magic of the waste :

A useless glitter, a resplendent void,
That charms the sight, but aches the bone and blood.
Nay—not so fast—why wilt thou cavil still,
Why murmur at what it is? What were this globe,
Were 't mantled not from this wide source with modes,
Refrigerant, to cool the burning zones,
And shed its nerving nodes the parching frame.
'Tis the north-star. Is he invincible?
O'erhead so near, his nadir—can it be.—
Cannot be reached? It must be, yet, it must.
Thou lesser light o'er all the lights distinct,
Distinguished glorious, whilst thou giv'st thy glow,
Unostentatious, only them who seek
Intent! See sets, Arcturus ne'er he sets:
Thou never risest, nay—thou never mov'st.
Thou holdst thy place when all the stars around
The sphere are rolling. Thee—Arcturus—thee
Does circle reverent. All the stellar host
Make their obeisance, their beatitudes
Take up their march unceasingly, and sing
To thee obedient their proud symph'ny, while
They still encompass thee, but filled with awe
At unfamiliar distance, nor approach
Thee dare, forever, nearer to thy seat:
Thou art the magnet of their touch, the flame
Of all their eyes, that ne'er avert their looks.
Thou art alone; and tho' thou hast, perforce,
That vast companionship of stars, they are
Not with thee, nay, they are remote, apart
They follow thee. They speak to thee, but thou,
Thou answerest not ; thou wouldst be isolate,
Nor wouldst be questioned yet, nor wouldst return
Vain compliments. Thou bidst them to their track,
The orbs ; thou dwellst in cold serenity,
Nor pitiest aught, and sendst thy twin compeer,
Terrestrial Boreas, blustering, rude, and fierce,
To blow his threats and speed the vengeant skies.
Thou art the seaman's guide ; all lustres change,

Thou never : he points to thee, finds thee, there,
Where thou wast always, where thou'd ever been,
From generation still unchangeable,
To long-gone generations, ere the time
Man could behold thee. Where he is he knows,
And whither he shall go he is advised,
Soon as he sees thee. Thou, thou art his friend,
His benison, ev'n tho' thou terrifyst
One-half the world, and bindst in deathly chains
One-fourth the zones and chillst the wintry year.
Does Arcturus ne'er set, thou ne'er dost rise,
Nay—ne'er dost move. When all the rest is change,
Thou still art there, unchangeable, unmoved,
When all the orbs have vanished, come and gone.
And thou art modest, too, tho' so superb,
And shrinkst, and to be found thou must be sought ;
Ev'n bright Ceopella far thy beam outshines ;
Yet thy keen, searching, pale, and perilous eye
Denotes thy malison and ominous mood.
Thou art intangible—ah, can it be,
We cannot meet and nestle at thy foot?
Who will assail thy centre ? who invade
Thy dim retreat, and brave thy Ayrannous blight?
   The night is present ; all the Arctic wails
Deep thro' his bounds. The lingering twilight fades,
And is no more. All, all is darkness, yet,
Not dusk, but dim, ineffable, tho' bright,
But viewless equal, such fantastic gloom,
And evanescent tho' 'tis still the same.
The day hath long departed, long will stay.
When will he come ? As tho' he never would,
'Tis night, 'tis endless night ; as tho' the world
Had bade adieu and fled with all its life,
'Tis but one round of ceaseless solitude.
The slender star's light radiance, if it wake
One bright reflection mid the crystal maze,
Spontaneous caught, 'tis but to make the void
More palpable, more full, more truly felt,

And emptiness is seen, but naught beside.
In caverns, hyperborean, are they pent,
Who there have haunt; tho' such the open space,
It has no borders. Calm full oft the hours,
In such severe repose they wane and wane,
As the obscure befits, continuous built,
In features so forgetful, and in form,
As absence not remembered. Voiceless, too,
Full oft, and silent as the depths of time,
From which no oracles or anthems come.
Till now, when all th' imprisoned billows speak,
And grate harsh thunder with such awful notes,
As tho' from Hades, and perdition calls
From the abyss, convulsed and overthrown,
Gigantic loud, where giants shake and shriek
Still struggling, startling every ear that's oped,
Flagitious from th' interior, where they clank
Their terrible chains, but unrepentant still,
To bane condemned for crimes that have no type,
Defiance, accent and despair's response,
Combined in one dread syllable, in one
Huge exclamation, in one mighty voice,
Repellant, doleful, fearful, and profound,
Repeated far, such else there's none on earth;
Destruction's advent and his writhing end.
The direful groans of all the eternal globe
There centre, dread invective, dark laments;
The pangs of evil brings preposterous frames,
Tho' curbed, rebellious, uttering still revenge.
Such dismal changes oft afflict and warp
Dismal—yet not to them who only hear,
More than an empty fear, tho' terrific;—
The uniformity. But, now, there's peace,
The while th' auroral mists dispread the sky,
In pearly shafts disposed, vermilion—toned.
'Tis quiet, yet activity, the while
The pageant all the ambiency illumes,
Like twilight or the moon. The phantoms rise,

Like squadrons, navies, or foot phalanxes,
From zenith to horizon garlanded,
And fill th' ambiguous extasy, the scope
Incongruous vague, with beamy arches crowned.
Triumphal, where they move, and march, and fade.
The skies are peopled, but the stillness is
The deeper from the vast procession traced,
So voiceless and unpalpable, aloft.
The jubilee of shades, co frequent do
These marked hallucinations teem, as 'twere,
The visible heav'n's consistent, native state ;
But now the shadows fleet, and wont prevails.
Oh night ! thou art a grateful change, thou givst
The weary rest, thou lull'st in halcyon dreams
The too long wakeful, and time's circle speed'st
With blest variety to most ; but here,
Thou'rt a misnomer, or non-entity :
No alternating day is thine ; it shines
Not on thy boundaries, it heralds not
Thy daily coming forth, nor harbingers,
Thy soon departure thence, thou art conformed
Of months, not hours, a too long, long repose,
That is not such, but torpor, and a chain
Of penalty the sinews to confound !
Tho' fish the deeps rove, and th' amphibia dwell
Productively, no living voice is heard.
The wild beasts have no utterance, they are stilled
In consternation, and their lips are shut,
Saved the tamed quadrupeds, when they are pricked,
Or feel the lash's touch, they yelp, howl and bark,
When they discover bait and find the spoil,
The while the glooms prevail, these shadows roam,
Celestial shed. As when man's tongue denies
Its wont expression, and he hides amid
The fall of empires and the wreck of hosts,
O'erawed and speechless ; or, as when, less marred
But fearing more. some boding meteor glares,
Precursor of events to come obscure,

Transcendant, which none may define, but still
Expects mysterious, while he trembles dumb.
Seldom the vapours are, the concaree's clear
But not transparent. All is shadowy, but
The shadows are not aqueous, only thus,
Etherial, of the ether. All is light,
But light that is not vision, a single hue,
That dims all others, and itself deflects
Into phantasma, or annulled absorbs;
And naught is real save th' all present Frost,
And the deep stars that glitter—doubly fair.
  What hails the pilgrims, now? The Esquimaux
Vociferating, with repeated shouts,
Approaching. Are they friendly, or at war?
Lyman meets Yocum, there, a forward chief,
Above his mates in stature, on the ice,
And beckons him. He understands and goes
With him aboard the ship. The rest remain;
But now invited thither, forward throng
Their teams abreast, with three-score bounding dogs
Beset and drawn from forth the hiding lodge.
They enter in, the animals lie down;
The guests have no design of ill 'twould seem.
But when their hosts them offer wheaten bread
And culinary luxuries, naught they'll eat,
Astonished haply at their naval trim,
In such unwonted quarters never known,
Yet not so venerating, they refrain
To touch all that does strike them, fore and aft,
And ransack, till they're held and bid away.
They will obey yet are felonious bent;
Their pilfering hands despoil of trivial goods
The lax establishment, a slender boat
Some leader takes with him, sore tempted by
The liqueous structure, when they do depart.
  Lyman will not be stern, and favors them.
He makes them presents, they bestow him game:
Thus, they may do when his provision fails,

Their hunt successful when his own may flag,
From their more full acquaintance more secure.
He treats with them; but when they soon return,
Their pledges they renew them and confirm.
   Yocum returns with his full company,
And gifts are interchanged. The visitors,
They promise venison, and seal, and furs,
To furnish them, and keep them oft informed;
Lyman gives payment. slight, but valued sorts
To them, and most of all to be desired.
Their garments are of mingled white and blue,
The fox's varied felt, a warm capote,
And trousers of the bear's wrap loins and feet,
With all his finny claws, on which they walk.
Armed for the frequent hunt they wield their knives,
With blades hoop-iron, and their lances, horn
The staff, but edged the point with sharpened steel,
Effective, which they bartered in the South,
At Uppernavick. Their fleet sledges are
Of walrus bone, the polished runners framed
Of finest ivory; the racy rim they glide,
Like wheels on golden axles lubricate.
Now they depart enjoined and jubilant,
Not emptily adown the crystalline,
Sped like the wind the bounding train alert:
They dwelt some three-score leagues and odd remote,
From the far harbour where th' explorers halt.
Some stellar cycles turn, a youth arrives,
And featly furnissned in his rapid car.
What wouldst thou, wild and rugged roving youth,
Yet gentle as a youth; what wouldst, alone
Mid these, so alien to thee? Wouldst thou bid
Them hence and haste away from these domains,
Thy rude forefathers' and thy own, which none
Should hold to thy distrust and detriment,
And leave thee thy bleak realm, by all refused
Till thou adopted it, and mad'st thy home?
Or wouldst expostulate with them to go?

Or wouldst thou stay with them, amd beg them take
Thee in, to live a more ennobled life?
  The query him about the recent theft,
The India rubber boat turn torn up, and reft
Of all its wood. He knows not nor repents.
Then, they confine him to the hold ; he sobs
In deepest grief subdued, nor will be soothed.
He does refuse the viands ; now, he sings
A simple stave, and now, he talks and cries.
Thus he laments till t'ward the midnight, then,
He lifts the hatch, and flees, and hath escape,
Before they omen or could overtake,
Were they disposed : the venturous bird is flown ;
The wild intruder shuns the bold event,
He will not wait. What follows his surprise.
His name is Folik, he will come again,
Yet not for months, and none of all his tribe
For weeks, tho' promising supplies, full oft.
  Long, long the night, the total night endures.
The Arctic couches an immeasured space.
No mortal eye his stature, length and breadth—
Can compass ever, where he bitter breathes,
But slumbers passive mid the blasting blight,
That fastens all to immobility,
And into stillness and to death transmutes.
But, now, the twilight hails, once more, tho' slow
Still wider it advances. Now, the sun,
The half forgotten sun, departed long,
And yet the more desired the more he seems
Well nigh extinguished—now the welcome orb
The fair horizon touches, now he greets
The dormant North, but scarce awaking yet,
And, ah, how slowly he broadens o'er the verge,
How tardily he rises from the bound !
Scarce notable his progress, Nature waits,
Impatient, for his presence unreserved,
And open countenance from East to West,
Illuminated. Now the day and night

Return like-measured, while in Aries' fields
He girds his coursers. Now, he greets the Pole
And rouses the Arctic. All that live rejoice.
Alas! his pow'rful aid is yet too wan,
Too far and brief to work his great behest!
His ardor pales before it well hath pierced
Th' intractable and thrice consolidate
Emergency. But yet benificence
He trebly brings; all th' outer Arctic lends,
Or must allow. The hybernating bear
He liberates, the fish he measures light;
The earth he fructifies with liquid springs,
Predominant, and gives the plumy race
Their northern territory undeterred:
He sheds the slender herbs their fleeting thrift
While man, who there inhabits or detains,
He brings redemption from the cold that kills,
Warmth, comfort, sustenance, and aid and cheer,
Where'er these yet are possible, or not
Quite alienate from th' unrelenting realm,
Obstreporous, and but by violence taught.

Behold, the Polar bear. With ardent weight
And quick celerity he stamps; it breaks,
The thickened ice, as by an avalanche
Of pointed virulence impelled and rent.
In pendant icicles his locks arrayed,
They glitter in the radiance' bounteous folds.
He laps his eager palate in his ire,
And finds his nutriment, that comes to seek
Th' inspiring atmosphere too long denied.

What tender care, what marked solicitude,
Employs the female's breast, maternal tied,
Ev'n like the tears of human sorrow shed!
She battles for her young and by them dies;
She feels warm instincts, tho' the frozen breeze
Encompass her. There, does she turn athwart,
To bring the spoil her cubs. Already, there,
Ah me? the hunter aims his fatal darts,

And both fall speedy dead. She starts and moans,
And places meat before them; naught they move.
The spoilers aim at her that tempts so near;
The leaden missive is no sport, and she
Is deeply wounded. Thrice she limps away;
As oft returns. She raises up her brood.
She licks them and entices them to walk,
But to her soft entreaties they are cold.
She moans, she cannot bear them off with her,
And now she turns a deathly glance her foes,
With understanding fraught: a deepened growl,
She by them dies, unshrinking to the last.
   Oft on the glaring plain the liquid seal
Drowses, a shortened hour. The ebb and flow
Of th' oceans palpitating 'neath his bonds,
Must have their respiration in the deeps,
Most sunless fettered. There the fluctuate tides
Have breathing space 'mid the thickest rime,
And open waters tho' of slender girth.
And there th' amphibia find their refuge sure,
From their profound imprisonment beneath.
Ofttime a single seal reposes, thus,
By these walled fountains, on their closest brink,
Thence issuing for a variance in his mode
Of life, else subterranean. Oft, thereby
The bear is watchful when the sun has ris'n,
Prone on his navel and his victim grasps,
But sometimes misses fitly. Here is one:
Foreboding wakes he, and looks up, but notes
Naught save such hummocks as have there their wont.
One feature favors him; the hunter, too,
Has on him aim as well 's the ursine watch;
His matchlock clicks, it does not burn, the prey
That instant drops and plunging disappears:
His ears are sharper than his filmy eyes.
The emulating twain go each their way,
Disgusted mutual at the frail attempt,
Nor will they now each other's valor try:

This will not brave the battle piece, nor that
Exemplify the beast's ferocious paw.
Abounds the summer sun, they crowd in flocks
The bordering shores around the open floods,
The smooth sea lions, minor, gentler forms
Of that proud bestial cognomen, and there,
The cautious boatman oft may overtake,
And sacrifice a score in agile guise,
And knock them facile down with clubs and blows.
 Come we to shipboard where the wanderers bide.
There Bynam sings, the cusinier, and still
Is lively, when the others oft are dull.
I cheerful am, tho' every gloom abounds;
And I will sing, tho' storms may rage without.
Still glad am I, howe'er the winter low'rs,
Will be alert, howe'er the frost benumbs,
And sing the strains of distant lands, where once
My footstep roved, but now is far avaunt,
Nor haply more will come. I will be cheered;
And stray where'er I may remember them,
And hope to near them if I shall not reach.
I will be grateful while the darkness winds;
I will rejoice, and be content, the while
There is enough, nor better can be found.
Nay, I will sing the songs of other lands
Than these, and think of them where'er we roam;
I will be cheerful still, and gladen oft,
Whate'er may fail for every bliss remains:
Let me but find my comrades hopeful, yet;
But if they languish, I will strive and sing.
His harmless ditty, thus, the purveyor trills,
Full many a time, amid th' unchanging hours.
 Now Ingreim, too, the sailor, breathes his last,
By hard tetanus seized and locked his chine,
Framed from his frozen limbs that would not heal.
They bury him by Otis; side by side
The twain repose in cold and stony graves.
But not till highest sun re-moulds the fixed,

Invulnerable ground, they build their cairen,
High-piled and steadfast o'er the force of twine,
With varied boulders from the confines rent.
Restored to-day, but not the less intense
The biting winds, ev'n tho' the snows dissolve
In favorite aspects, where the warmth may wedge,
Resistless 'mid the crispy molecules,
Th' inmates go forth, prospective, and survey
The heights, the plains, anew, the bright expanse,
The ofttime indentations; thus prepare
For longer search towards the Pole designed,
When the fit season best rewards the pains.
  In varied parties they divide their list,
While some remain. Some to th' interior toil;
Some drive the briny border, some across
The solid billows to the sunset shore,
While some the friendly aborigines
Seek out, and new acquaintanceship become,
Adown the solemn gulf where'er they dwell.
  Here, the three-brother turrets, like the trace
Of obelisks in Egypt found, and thence
To other lands transported, save that these
Immovable and mightier are, they meet.
Here peaks of burnished crysolite and mounds
Of fluent silver in its mould congealed,
And ridges of chalcedony, with sides
Far polished and expanding far as th' eye,
And glaciers on the continent, which are
High mountains. There a slender shaft
Uprises like a tow'r, proportional,
But higher, steeper, such the deepest snows
Cannot invade it, or take hold the frame,
A bare-bound beacon 'mid the silent gorge,
Of green stone moulded, flagged with limy schist;
And there the granite peers among the crags,
Athwart th' impending drift of thousand years.
  'Yond by the coast they mark bold headlands, oft,
Far capes and glittering heights, and ragged cliffs,

O'erbeetling now and threatening overfall
Most frequent, timely, then receding, or
Precipitous, deep inlets and slight bays,
Or magnified, still marked where'er they dip,
By strong abutments all the outline edged.
So architectural is all the view,
Yet vast and warped, as tho' the Cyclops here,
Had wrought as well as in the Orient, save
'Tis the Fire's absence here, and all is Frost,
Frost, the sole presence which the marvel makes.
   More would they know of these vast intervales;
But most these brief excursions do they drive.
Preliminary, and preluding but, to inure
Suchwise their seasoned joints unhinderingly,
Accomplished thus in manner best to win
The greater objects in their chief intent.
   Clouds interrupt the ether now for days,
And vapors form more frequent. Now the snows
Accumulate ; this moment, dumpy, dank,
They fall, continued long, but quietly.
No breezes move ; 'tis still as 'twere a shade,
And deep incumbrances full sure they prove,
And wide deposits scarce the summer rids.
How oft these amplified, thick show'rs impede
The outward marches ; oft the invaders sink,
Scarce t' extricate them from the flabby toils !
Then, later, when the daily, constant sun
Shines months, unsetting, and the stellar crale
Arrests his up ascent and bids him pause,
To turn him back—then fogs immense arise,
And mantle th' earth and air ; a brooding haze
Envelopes th' atmosphere and robes the view,
And mystifies the distances, tho' naught
But these adverse phenomena obstruct.
'Tis still, and yet 'tis cutting, raw and drear.
But now the deep-winged gales unchecked advance,
And sweep them momently from all the space,
Significant and total, nullified,

Like cobwebs by a besom from the sight,
Where they entangle th' eye and mar th' expanse.
  Impetuous-driven, now, another snow,
But storm-united, intervenes and wails,
And pierces them that brave it. Where no night
Comes round, 'tis darkness; where the sun doth shine
From morn to eve, from eve to morn, nor sinks,
Within the sky set ceaseless all the hours,
'Tis Boreal Winter. Yet the spell is o'er,
By the next change the tempest now assumes,
It turns itself and settles into calm,
And the cold sunshine hues the drifted hoards.
  At Eider island, o'er the level plane
Of frozen waves, but far beyond the scope
Of vision, at the most transparent phase
Of answering light, the migratory tribes,
The feathery habitants, have made their haunt,
Each year repeated. Now they harbor there,
In flocks, gregarious, vast, beyond belief;
The eider's down, of all the finest down,
And fit for fairies' pillows, there is grown;
And later, when the summer 'gins to shrink,
The eider's young is grown mature and plump,
A countless horde amid the rocks and heights,
Oft inaccessible and icy-barred,
Like pictures variegate, and pinnacled.
There feed the cormorants upon the brood;
The sweeping gulls feast on them. All have homes
In vicinage; as well the ungainly auks.
Yet that delicious plunder, none they note,
Save the dam, haply, such the multitudes
There flourish and so bountiful are reared.
  Just when the Pilgrims find the far retreat,
'Tis at this season when the inmates hold
Their social saturnalia, and delight
In holiday, till they remove from thence.
They carry with them much as they can bear,
Caught easy of this palatable store,

And were it near would furnish fresh resource
Of sustenance, to answer mouth to mouth,
A sanitary diet for scurvied lips.
Lyman and Christeansen are here the guests:
But on the bending ice the sledge breaks in,
And Lyman from the rubbish scarce escapes
The open water, immingled insecure,
While his companion, terror-stricken, vows,
Invokes, and makes the amplitude appeals.
 The eider makes on cliffs his downy nest,
But here he builds o'er all the craggy grounds.
The eider nestles in the edging cliffs,
But bathes the billows far below his roost,
And lives upon the breakers, never tired,
From hour to hour, and sinks or swims at will.
And finds his provender by all the coves.
The eider dwells amid the rugged reefs
And chilly winds, but yields the softest bed
And warmest bolster to the fondled child
Of ease and luxury, all the realms afford:
The eider spares his foe full oft his young,
But yet is numerous o'er the sternest North.
This island shore toward the evening lies.

BOOK IV.

ANGELICAL.

Morn comes no more, nor eve ; they stay aloof
And passive, in their covert domicile.
   The Esquimaux provide their wintry stores,
The plunder of the sea and th' inland glades,
Most sun-enfolded, and frost-sheltered haunts.
They bring the turfy mosses, earth-congealed,
Like plastic stones, the roofs of recent huts,
Or more dilapidate, to deck secure,
And shelter from the penetrating winds.
   In his not inefficient foresight prides
The native lord of all the boundlets realm,
The sure possessor if such ownership
Where scarce there's aught but sole the elements,
Reft of their accessories save the sea's,
Can have existence or be thus affirmed.
   In th' earth but seldom he his tenement builds,
For 'tis impermeable. Of rended rocks
And plied interstices, he measures it ;
The wall, the vestibule, the roof are such.
Or oft of rimy blocks he rolls and piles
The massive snow, and makes a roomy berth,
Ev'n at his wish, secure and tempest-tight.
Or, on the ice he frames a crystal house,
Out o'er the sea of ice-connected walls,
And, like one solid boulder, void a flaw,
With limpid panes like glass for windows set,
By the congealing flood supplied in nooks,

Peculiar placed, whereby far out he sees
And hath abundant light. But with the night
These lessen hourly and are soon no more ;
Like fairy structures, when the morning beams,
They vanish in the summer ; they who dwell
Evacuate them at a timely date.
His hearth, his bowl, are bone ; his chafing dish
A stone diminished to a fitting frame,
And like an altar they command a place,
His fuel, oil, he burns it and he eats.
His armor is the arrow, spear and lance ;
His bow the thong of hides, and so his lash,
Whereby he drives his rapid-running team.
His robe impervious furs, he goes abroad,
Nor dreads the beating drift nor pinching air.
His habitation is the billow, when
Its loins are free, and there his bending float
He launchs and rides, and finds his fare and life.
 Once on a time a guest to Umah came,
A radiant form, and far beyond he seemed.
In likesome shape and native graces blessed,
All other mortals they had ever seen,
Who therein dwelt. And they invited him
To their best viands he would not partake,
And said he needed naught. Soon he departs.
Then Oniah to her sister Nanga says,
"It was an angel's." "Oh, what meanest thou ?
An angel-Oniah, thinkest thou the like,
An angel would come here ?" cries Oniah then.
"An angel came to them were humble too,
As well as we ; why should he not come here ?"
"And thou rememb'rest what the father read,
That late informed us, from the book wherefrom
He taught us lessons, how the angels spake
With human beings." Oniah thus replied.
The elder answered : "'Twas in th' ancient times :
But, Oniah, now they do not visit them."
"If they that are so far above ourselves

Believe, why should we doubt? Ev'n of our tribes,
There are who deal in mysteries, and have
High pow'rs to heal or harm by spirits giv'n,
Which in another world than ours exist.
Thou knowest, Nanga, there's another world,
And spiritual pow'rs from thence we do invoke,
Exalted over us, which all confess."
The younger thus, at which the sister said,
And turned away—"Oh! surely, yes, there are
Both good and evil spirits, too, but thou
Mayst be content, they will not visit us!"
  Again the stranger came ; ev'n as they turn
He stands before them, but so gently calm
Is he, such mildness in his countenance,
They lean toward him, glad, but Oniah most.
He understands their speech ; his words are few,
But meaningly are uttered, and he speaks
Of gentle skies and Heav'n. When he departs,
Such kindly gifts to Oniah he bestows,
As she would always prize, but cherish now,
Beyond their common value. Soon, again,
To their acceptance he presents himself ;
And now the subject he dilates upon,
Is heav'nly love and human. How the Lord
Of all creation lends mankind his gifts,
And cares to draw them to'ard their better state,
And sends salvation in their utmost need,
And how good men have sacrificed their all,
To bring blest tidings, and to teach the means
To them who live unfavorably, remote,
Or lost to renovation and relief,
Of being happy, happier than they'd been,
Without this intercession and this care,
Wrought by heav'n's ministers their fellow man,
In love to him above, ev'n their own life ;
And for the praise of God, who gives them joy :
And bow to them ev'n in the colder North,
To which they were but ill habituate ;

They came, devoted, by such love inspired.
Such was his theme. They hear him edified,
But nearest still t' Oniah his address,
Who hears him most perceptive and akin.
  Now, frequent he sojourns, yet only brief
His stay is, and no inmate he becomes,
And food at times partakes he, or he tastes ;
But oftenest he refrains. He has enough,
Or seemeth so to have, or needeth none,
And only takes as tho' t' approve the mode,
Still gentle while his glorious features speak.
Thus while the winter's imminent not, he makes
His presence there a moment, or an hour,
Or haply too a day his haste prolongs.
  At one such interval when he is gone,
Thus Oniah muses by the rude, rough ledge :
Out in the restless surge the fishes swim ;
The soaring kittiwakes among the crags,
Their nurslings nurture, and the beasts have range
They had not earlier. I am glad whene'er
The stranger meets us ; in his absence lone,
But hope for him to bring us joy again.
Yes, he is fair, and bountiful is he,
As is the warming sun more so than man,
And wiser than all mortals. How serene,
As the white morning when the day ascends,
And the strong ices 'gin to break their frame ;
As the red evening when the midday sinks,
And the sharp breezes weave their sooner chains.
I see him ever. By the shining beach
I stand, he is before me ; on the plain,
He is beside me ; in the cabin's fold,
He calls, he knocks, he comes. Where goest thou—
Ah ! whither, Oniah ? Wilt go with the guest ?
Will he take thee with him ? Will he accept
Thy frail attendance to celestial climes ?
Where wouldst thou stay? Here? Wouldst thou proffer
    him

A home when bleaker seasons grow to freeze?
Wouldst thou invite him to be entertained,
Or stay with *thee* and ever to forget
His angel origin, his home divine?
Would he be recreant to his blissful kind?
Would he abide with thee, and ne'er turn back?
And if he would, then, could he thus his place
Abandon, and for me thus heav'n resign?
No, neither. He will come as his own mind
Allows, and so go hence ; a blessing still,
His every feature when his form appears,
As to the latent germ too chilly thralled,
The sunny beam ; and when his presence ends,
I shall be grateful and recall the past.
Ye kittiwakes, that in the distance sport,
Within mine eye-sight happy. Ye can take
Your wing and speed where'er ye list, while we
Must build slow vehicles, or slowly wend,
Or trust the treacherous element, or climb
The wandering heights. Oh, that your wings were mine!
 Provided by a portable mess, now meets
Her sister, Naugwin, and cries : "Oniah, hail!
Why stay'st thou thus among the slopes so long?"
"The rigorous winter will be long enough ;
We need not shun the sunshine, where 'tis fraught
The fullest," says she that had been addressed.
Naugwin returns : "Our brother thee'd not have
Be lone, so long continued 'mid the wild,
So far away, and says thou shouldst return,
Or have companions." "Let him be at peace ;
Long as our father yet is satisfied,
He need not be concerned and troubled thus,"
Oniah then answers. "No—he need not be,
But is ; yet thou wilt not with me refuse
To be attended, wilt thou? Let me tell ;
Our father purposes a new device,
And thou art not informed, since thou went out,
Broached only—purposes to build

A palace on the ice, our winter's home,
To be constructed when his arrows threat,
'Twill be a novel trait, a beauteous change."
Thus Naugwin question made, and Oniah said :
"As he disposes I am well content."
"But should the stranger," Naugwan now replies.
"Arrive with us, thou wilt be quite remote."
"Mayhap," the sister answers, "not so far
I should be, or than ye he would be near
To me or nearer, or would meet me first."
To which the other : "But thou wilt come back :
Or wilt thou stay with me yet longer here?
Why wilt thou be alone?" Then Oniah said :
"Either way, as thou lik'st ; I do not urge
To be thus by myself engaged, except
It happen thus, nor is there aught to bid
Me still remain ; yes, we will now return."
Then the twain took their distance to the lodge.

 Next at the cottage when the guest arrived,
He told of th' angels, and of th' angel's loves.
And said he those benignant are so filled—
For there are two sorts, those to evil bent,
As well as these—so filled with love they would
With mortals share their own felicity,
And thus descend ev'n from their blest estate.
To meet on earth and join in earthly ties.
In olden ages they came down from heav'n,
To dwell with mankind oft, and thus would knit
Relations hymenial, and take them wives
Of human membership. They would so yet ;
Since thus they're fraught with love intense, and pure,
Surpassing all terrestrial; and which is
Their nature's essence. Thus they have a rank
'Tween earth and heav'n, and thus they too would bless
Humanity. Because they're interfused
With the *divine* so amply, thence they give
To them with whom they form a league a part
Of their divinity, and wish the same,

And hope to aid the needy, and to raise
The fallen up from their too low decline,
Which they had less deserved than many else.
Such ties they would not need, nor cares they own,
But cherish them, since others thus they lead
To fuller blessing, and are blessed themselves.
Such-wise, the more, by their expanded love,
That yet scarce owns an element of self.
Yet, did they sometimes lose, and later put
To hazard greatly their own innocence,
Or native eminence, and virtual worth,
Forgetful of their true integrity,
And merged in baser memories, heav'n annulled.
Thus Passion grew bereft its heav'nly flame,
Degenerate, and they were punished by
The Cherubim for their alliances,
Their fond alliance with the tribes of men,
And were condemned to earthly bondage, like
The earthly races, shut out from above,
To mortal dissolution subject, as
The denizens of this sublunar world,
For whom they forfeit their etherial birth.
Such was the result, since they fell; they erred,
Not since they came to earth, and then bestowed
Their benefactions, nor because they made
Such joint connections and too much diverse,
And shared their nature with the child of man,
And gave their gifts to it, by mercy taught
And love angelic—no—but since they threw
Those glorified advantages away,
Forgotten, lost—and they were human sole;
And none could find in them aught than the wont,
Nor could bestow else than they born on th' earth,
To all its vast discrepancies confined
Were they like all, henceforth: they should have watched,
Which was not need to do there whence they came,
Or, at the least, the more was needful here.
And further said he. Nor does he, in truth,

Receive less blessing than he giveth them,
And man bestows the angels happiness,
Thus, by this love impassioned and conjoint.
They for companionship full often yearn ;
They too enjoy a change, and do not lack
A subtle sense for much variety.
Since oft from their potential state dismissed,
Between the planets or the solar orbs.
On distant missions ; more especially
When on the earth demanded are they plied
By such conditions. Can they but retain
Celestial influence, and in wane of time,
Return to their indigenous abode,
They're not averse, nay, gladden to be joined
In temporary bonds upon the earth :
Superior they, but yet they find their like,
Amid th' unlike in mankind, contrast fair.
By the divine tho' less are these infused,
'Tis the same spirit which, more, less, in each
Irradiates, and soul can speak to soul ;
If but a spark illumine, that is light
With light concordant, and commingle they,
In fond communion and attachment sweet.
The greater with the least, howe'er diverse
Their aspects else, the soul is kindred, thus,
And those receive a high regard from these ;
These pity from the others and fond care :
And thus they owned a passionate desire
For the fair children of the earth confessed,
The angels, in those ages long agone ;
And since they have descended, too, at times,
And formed re-union with such mortal loves.
Thus Uriel—so they called him since he told
Them now his appellation—did inform
Their lacking apprehension. When he went,
Departing, Oniah gazed, long after him :
She gazed : he faded like a vision thence,
From the view gradually, yet all too soon,

And so complete as tho' he had not been.
Whene'er they have their habitations yond,
They may descend to us, and they may dwell
With us, and lend us aid ; the angels love,
And they may bring us blessings, oft, to them
If we adhere, nor grieve them from our side.
Not only evil spirits here there are,
But the celestial ; these may hold with those
An equal contest. Can we be arrayed
But with these, gracious, we need never be
O'ercome by th' others ; and they too will form
A union with ourselves, and join our lot,
When their devotion calls them to this bound,
Since still dependent on the pow'r on high,
And subject to th' ineffable commands.
And this is he, this—Uriel is the one
Of them, come hither ! Let me now rejoice.
The storms awake, the frozen vapors loom ;
The sweeping snows they gather up their show'rs
Repeatedly, the sun looks dim and dull,
And wanders farther hence, but I have joy,
And gladness thrills me more, still more than wont.
Let me entreat the stranger still to stay,
And let me beckon to him yet to come ;
Let me invite him to the drooping couch
And slumber, when 'tis cold, nor bid him fly,
Nor let him go away when winter wails,
And to the downward night the day declines.
Oh ! shall he prove to have a kindred soul,
And love the dying, piteous, let me call
The guest to festival and human cheer !
The breezes are too brisk, the fringed clouds
Are ominous, a half a day at most,
The skies are clear again, the wastes are bright,
The evening yet serene, full oft returned.
The angels love, and Uriel too, he, too,
May love ; he is an angel ! Uriel come,
Come, nor refrain thy coming, oft, so long.

Oh, stay! oh! do not quite away remain!
At last, at last, thou'lt come no more; at last,
The angel comes no more, he goes away,
And stays, forever gone; but I rejoice!
But I rejoice he ever present was,
And will be glad whate'er thereafter brings.
  Thus Oniah broke into a grateful chord,
And sang till by the chilly drift advised.
  An altered mood in Oniah now appears;
More graceful, joyful, and more beautiful,
She seems, than ever known, so altered now,
As tho' 'twere not herself, the form the same,
But changed the features to such gentleness,
That was a novelty could none but note
Th' illumination sweet, and when the guest
Is present, all her countenance reflects
A light unwonted. Now, his presence, there,
He makes, again, apparent; in the hut
They now familiarize, and half converse,
And partly muse, impent, till now they drop
Into a sleep of halcyon somnolence,
And nightly depth, such as the night deploys,
And simple weariness to rest that lulls.
How long was their repose were none to mark,
But when they woke the angel guest was gone.
He had departed, none knew how or when;
Nor had awakened he of one the heed,
Ev'n dreamily, that any one had stirred,
And least, gone from the lodge, that was so close
Impounded and shut up 'twould wreak a noise,
To go from thence. More warily none could,
Than so to make no stir that some would hear.
  Drawn to the outer verge where they prepared
To frame their winter-warding domicile,
The faithful mother and the daughters stand
Upon the firm-bound ice, as tho' they were
In council o'er the wisdom of the plan.
Awhile they pause, since now the waning skies

Are calm and soothing, tho' the slanting night
Approaches steadily, that is, the day
Is setting; yond the scarce perceptive hill
The sun is out of view, but hath not set.
Yet now the twain alone the mother leaves,
And wends her path direct toward the home.
  Upon the ice alone the maidens wait,
And point the round horizon's varied points,
To note the more informal phase of all
The circumambient ether, seemingly.
And now they are sedate, toward the west
Their glances fixed, and are immovable.
  "How radiant is that border!" Oniah says.
"How splendent is the way that yonder leads!
Naugwin, methinks the angels there may dwell."
"Mayhap they do," this answers; "but I ween,
If ever they come down the earth upon,
The morning brings them, and with him do they
Come hither; 'tis more fit, the morning glads,
The evening saddens, oft, and sheds us gloom,
If gloom there be, the most of all the hours."
"Ah—thinkest thou—perhaps, at times, but yet
The evening charms beyond that gayer light!
And is it not eternity, we see
Therein depictured far, how pure, how deep,
How heav'nly colored with serenest rays?"
"Not less I'd choose the dawn, dost thou not oft
Declare to me the angels come to bless,
And bring us gladness, joyful like the morn?"
"Their haunt is 'mid the stars and etherward,
They may hail in the midnight, at the noon;
But there I do believe they congregate,
And hold their laudant jubilee and sing
Their grateful songs, and praise the great Supreme,
At the eternal gates, the gates of heav'n."
"And thou would'st hold thou see'st the very doors
Of that blest region?" "That beatitude
I see, there is no end, and such is theirs,

Unlimited. Hath not the father told
Us, oft, they dwelt in purer light, more fair,
Than all created else, an endless grace,
Nay, in beatitude? And this is it,
The image of beatitude, at least,
The shadow hither cast if nothing more ;
And, then, it must be bordering there, if not
The benison, itself—think'st thou not so?"
"It may or may not be, I do not know ;
I cannot guess so far and certainly :
But see, the glooms prevail, that lucent gloom
Is paling, now, they draw its glories down
To darkness and to nothingness absorbed.
There is no more ; let us now go from hence,
Full soon, and ere the lonely night o'ertakes."
"A ruddy evanescence—oh, 'tis there,
But now 'tis vailed—yes, we will now depart!"
So did the twain reiterate, and hold
A slight debate ; then took their twilight path.
 Dim dawns the dusk, and with slow, lingering step
The night advances ; but a shortened space
He now obscures the noon, when Uriel hails,
In sobered yet in half divergent mood,
That wont to be so open and composed,
And Oniah greets he by the ledge abroad.
 Enwrapt in wint'ry furs are each ; the air
Is searching, now, ev'n by the midday sun,
And Uriel thus the listening maid bespeaks :
."'Tis the last privilege. I now must forth :
My mission calls me hence, and at an end
Is my vocation here. I come to take
Departure final, they who sent me bid
Me now to take my needful station else.
Would'st thou go with me, Oniah? Would'st thou, then,
Accomp'ny me to quite another sphere,
Than this in which thy days have ever grown?"
"Oh! I would go with thee, but am aware
I am not fitted else to dwell, remote,

And severed from my wonted paths, but yet
Thou know'st the best, I do ev'n as thou say'st!"
Thus, she replies, and Uriel then resumes:
"Nay—thou art not prepared; it must be so,
That thou shouldst here remain and I depart.
But be not then alarmed because we met,
And do not always meet; think not 'tis ill,
But a blest bounty, that we could be joined
A season, in this wild, accompanied,
Since 'tis the devious nature of my task,
To change locality and be transferred.
Perchance, I shall in other days return,
But this is yond my ken; meanwhile think but
Of me as of one such that must have been
But for a time, and let not aught disturb
Thy balanced memory to bid thee grieve,
But gladden since there was an added life,
Ev'n tho' not lasting. Follow what may woo
Thee to advantage, maugre all that was,
And do believe what ill may loom o'er all,
'Twas not the greater but the less from thence,
And what high good may come 'twas thus so great,
And not diminished from that former cause.
Yet, if I evermore, again, should hail
These greeting shores, be sure I seek thee out,
And I shall find thee wheresoe'er thou art;
And haply then thou, willing and prepared,
May'st be to follow me, and go from hence
In other hours, so prospered if thou wouldst.
But now accept these tokens of regard,
In fit remembrance held of him who'd been.
But for a time, these rare, regardful gifts,
In memory of him thou met'st, full oft,
But didst not meet for always, as tho' dead."
  "Oh! must thou go immediate, thus, and canst
Not stay awhile, yet linger, but must haste
To part abrupt, so instant and unwarned."
  Oniah rejoins, and Uriel answers mild:

"Nay, 'tis an order cannot be annulled,
As fixed as that sun's course, I am dismissed,
And I must go whatever else may hap,
This moment, but prolonged this interchange,
The counsels which I serve bear no suspense,
But when I yonder come, my prayers shall be
To heav'n, to lend their aid and peaceful joy;
And if my true petition may prevail,
Thou wilt be blest yond what thou otherwise
Couldst ever be, much as the earth's fold allows.
And now farewell—a grief—but soon 'twill cease:
Oniah, farewell—a grief, but greater bliss,
T'ave been, t'have had, the privilege—farewell!"
"Farewell—I do believe and am content,"
She said, and ceased. No word, and Uriel flees
Immediate-swift. And long her fastened eyes
On his departure Oniah fixes, far.
Now halts he, turning, and he makes a sign
Of recognition yet, and lifts his palm
Ascending, reached, then vanishs undenied,
As by a mist enveloped; all is bleak,
And gone where late he stood, o'er all th' expanse.
"Alas! 'tis o'er, and now alone I am;
Uriel is now no more, to heav'n ascends.
How shall I spend the vacant time, how brave
The scowling skies, how bear the long night's weight?
The midnight loneliness, and be at peace!
I am alone, but not forgotten, yet;
Uriel hath been. 'Twill be a joy, that c'er
His presence hath been mine, that e'er he stayed.
I will be glad, tho' gloomy, and rejoice,
Tho' sorrowing, since his absence must become.
Tho' vanished, tho' afar, he is not lost.
It was an angel; now an angel, he
A friendly angel is, felicitous,
Not less that here he strayed: whate'er my step
Admonish, and whatever pains be mine
To suffer still, I know that he is blest

In that vicinity where blessing's rife,
And my well-being is suchwise the more.
My soul, oh, thither, when the frame expires!"
   Long pausing thus she plained, then back, forth, winds,
Slow, sauntering, to the cottage, half a void,
In thought abstracted, full of dreamy flights.
   A saddened mood the inmates do observe
In Oniah, now. Long night the day usurps,
Nor Uriel comes again. At last they broach
The subject, wondering why the stranger comes
No more, that wont so frequent there to pass
The fleeting moments. Then, first Oniah speaks,
And tells them he will come no more, and has
Ta'en leave forever. How she knows so much,
They still inquire, whom then she first informs,
He met her late, and 'twas the parting last,
Nor had to spare save that brief interview,
The time's mere instant urged to go at once,
Commanded by the Pow'r he must obey,
And Uriel, now, they'll find will come no more.
   When now the Spring returned, and scanty buds
Began to spring, the sun-encumbered nooks
Rejoicing tender mid the vaporate snow,—
A child was born t' Oniah, an angel boy,
(Tho' wedded not, a wife Oniah is)
Of goodly frame: they called him Folik, then,
The same who from the brig made his escape,
These few days since and would not be immured.
   "Folik"—that was his name—"not Folik, he
That unattended came, and from the ship
Escaped so opportune!" Lyman exclaimed,
When Yocum added, who the story told.
"The same," said Yocum. "Ah," the former cried,
"Had I but known the like he had not went
So easily from thence, ere we had done
Him some acknowledgment for his descent
And wondrous birth; but we must do so yet."
   'Twas at an entertainment waited by

The Esquimaux, this narrative occurred.
 Reverting to a not unalien theme,
Shall they not too be sung and claim the verse,
Who taught these terror-stricken wilds to glow
With human sympathies and gentler love?
 By Denmark planted first, here grew a seed
That bore good fruit; the Lutheran precedes,
And to his faith the native tribes converts.
But afterwards Moravia's borders led
The missionaries thither, introduced
By their forerunners. To th' interior pierced
These Brethren, far from all th' established pests,
Mid wastes before untrodden by the foot
Of civilized example. There they taught
The savages, and by unselfish acts,
Regardless of all other meet rewards
Than their benign intentions, which sufficed,
Inspired the wanderers, poor and vice-inclined,
With better dispositions and the love
Of higher truths than e'er they had conceived;
And thus persuaded them away to cast
Their idle superstitions and absurd,
And their degraded passions to amend.
Naught feared they aught the frigid-breathing Frost,
That killed all others, in their hallowed zeal,
But bore privations of all sorts the worst,
That had deterred all mankind else, rejoiced,
And braving pains too sore to be described,
And threading weary solitudes too vast
To be e'en imaged, never did they cease
Their toils benevolent and undefined,
Heroic patience, which bestowed the prize,
Till all the realm where'er the inmates dwelt,
Regenerate, with recent faith was filled;
Nor could them hunger, chill or death's self thwart.
 Since when they have a táste of grace, at least,
In those dominions froze, the dwellers there,
Tho' yet in part their olden rites retain

A portion, and t' incongruous spirits bend,
And false magicians hold their revels still,
They are ameliorate: at least a gleam
Of full intelligence pervades them all,
And aids to make their natural rigors less,
Themselves more gentle, what they bear less harsh,
And turns to benefit what else were harm,
Till, than some better placed they happier are.
  Let them have their true meed who do such deeds,
And work such true effects; let them be named
With honor and acknowledged by mankind.

BOOK V.

THE DREAM.

  With sportive games their simple leisure passed,
Such as befitteth men of tried emprize—
The royal chessmen drilled, or dice and cards—
And ofttime served while ceased the out employ,
Fair science, deeper labors to relieve.
  These were the principal, and most engaged
The ship's inhabitants. To draw the lines
Of measurements, and map the varied coasts,
And fix the place of continents and capes,
And isles and inlets with the winding seas;
To sketch the highlands and the glaciers wide

Delineate, and limn the boreal scenes,
And mark the temper which the weather takes,
In frequent changes that the bulb denotes,
Mercurial, what the skies proclaim, calm, clear,
Or tempest-beaten, frowning mid the shade
Of vapors gathering, snowy drifts, or rain,
Or smiling constellations and the orbs
Of fuller light, dispelling all the mists ;
To note the occulation of the stars,
And their conjunction, oft, at what degrees,
The moon's obliquity or absent phase,
Or corruscations of the moving night :
But most were they devoted to revolve
Their future marches, and their episodes
Of deviation, with, mayhap, the hunt,
And their provision's fullness best supplied,
And to compare their most consistent plans,
Most feasible, that were not always like,
For the completion ardent they desired,
Their pilgrimage's and rugged travail's end,
Indisputable, when they might repose ;
But chief this was the chieftain's to devise :
Thus were they occupied while idle else.
 The company are assembled, all the chief.
Lyman addresses them : " Now is the time
T' improve our vantages. Not only bold
But persevering we must be, immoved,
Tenacious, as the tendril to its grasp,
To our endeavored purpose let us cling
Unaltering ; thus we shall advance, alert,
And go the farther, be ev'n longer-lived.
The Pole is not too near, we yet may reach
Its central boundary not improbably,
So firm resolved. From such resolve, so fixed,
All difficulties shrink that met in mood
Diverse, were yond surmounting, to the best
Impossible. We have one object all ;
We'll share defeat or victory, and each

Will gather gloom or glory, win or lose.
We are as one, we flourish or we pale,
Together banded, living, dying, still,
Whatever threat, and that fast polar field,
Is as an enemy, would us debar
From our deserts so just our worthy meed.
Companions, let us be awake, at once ;
But have ye aught a difference to note,
Or whether ye are cordial in that beam,
Which my own vision strikes, let each declare
Unhindered, willing all to hear, we wait :
To my not undigested purport, how
Do ye reply, to us such weighty sort?"
  Spake Theobald. "It less deserves how far
We do proceed, than that we measure well,
Where'er we are. I deem we may, perchance,
Assume too much in hoping thence to reach
That inward or that outward mystery.
Yet do we but approach the vicinage,
We yet may cull most vital facts, collect
Great illustrations, nor be thence abashed,
Because we did not climb the uttermost.
Not since there's peril would I half desist
The farthest, since that peril less rewards,
So undertaken in the prospect thence,
So nearly sure a failure, yet so large,
So large expenditure, so slight a hope.
Let me assert near reckless thus 'twould seem,
To seek remotest, and mayhap neglect
The easy nearer, most attainable,
But a rash venture haply forfeit all.
Will it be vain, an enterprise so built,
Complete far as it goes, securing sure
A slender good, but certain? Trivial gifts
With little cost are oft to be preferred
To greater, coupled with such onerous weight
Of sacrifice, they turn to bane 'stead bliss.
Let me not be, I ask, misunderstood.

I say this much, but only to suggest :
Should ye be other-minded, I will throw
No lagging in the way, but with ye wend
Determinate and cheerful, one at heart ;
And should both be, the least and most, achieved,
I shall be doubly grateful, and fulfilled
My wish will be. Whate'er ye do decide,
And the commander bids, I ready am ;
For me, I will go far as one, but let
Us not forget the intermediate worth."
    Then the physician, Jarnie, moved and said :
"There will be more than one disabled thus,
And some left skeletons upon the road,
In reaching that lone distance, far and deep,
Or ev'n in nearing it, can there be such.
But be it simply possible, for one
I say, let it be tried whate'er th' event,
With all the innate energies combined,
That heav'n bestows, and skill that man commands.
I'm for th' experiment, my trusty friends,
And on me count, if but a gleam shine out
With promise hued, as in its favor full,
And the proposal has my strong assent,
And every aidance, wish, and will, and deed ;
A great disclosure, for its sure success
Abetting, hitherto unknown and hid,
And scarce one equaled were it now but grasped."
    At which Alphonso took continuous word :
"Superfluous 'twere to add to what hath been
So fitly said, the last ; in all their force
Those views are mine, and need no further speech."
    But Gerrit answers all : "Shall we proclaim
The feasible at first ? Shall we inquire
First, can the Pole be reached ? And shall we wait
Till we shall know ? We cannot know th' attempt
Until we make. The doubt must be resolved.
It cannot solve itself by being broached
In vague supposals. No—we must go forth,

And try undaunted. Then we partly prove,
Can it be done or not, and sooner not.
What can we urgent, more or less, than make
Th' endeavor, then? Why, that is all we can?
Not all the principalities of th' earth,
Not all the pow'rs of Pandemonium's self,
Shall ever hinder us from doing what
We can, and more we cannot. Can we find
Before we seek? And ere we do begin,
How can we end? Can we discover aught
Without the eye's acretion claiming sight,
Without the ear's propinquity, that claims
The hearing, to be audible or clear?
Nay—we must go there, if to ascertain
We do desire, or prove the effort false,
The trial futile, and the work in vain,
The race impossible, not to be won.
Let us be well provided, all that skill
Can best supply, and truest wits devise.
Then forward, fearless, far as limbs can move,
Nor ask the question can we go, who should
Be on the path to know, and never halt,
Till course accomplished or conditions balk,
Incontrovertible and not t' evade,
Not inward, but from outward; then we stop,
And only then: so shall we gain the most,
And if not all, one point arraign at least,
And gather honors of no common pith,
If not preëminent, the very Pole,
Ne'er faltering nor once thinking to desist,
While there's one mode, one prospect to avail."
 From the recess now Moulton calm advanced,
And the assembled in this sort addressed:
 "Vast are the spaces, and an amplitude,
That we would never ween with bounteous room
For millions of inhabitants, obtains.
That region whither we to go propose,
Is not a desert, but a fructuous zone,

If what I had cognition be not feigned.
I was transported there to me unknown,
That other night when slumber weighed us down
Together somnolent, all slept profound.
'Tis said by savans versed, the rounded globe
Is flattened at the Pole ; but 'tis much more.
'Tis like an excavation, so depressed,
Or hollowed spindle ; for th' internal scope
Is scooped out, hundred on still hundred miles.
I was transported there, and duly such
Was I astonished, scarce my joints would stir,
And speech had failed me had I sought to speak,
At the transition from this frozen realm,
To such a fertil bound and clement sky,
There where we deemed the frost the most extreme ;
Yet, from my stupor I recovered soon,
And 'gan to query, how or where is this ?
One was near by me, saw my puzzled mood,
And marked confusion ; then to me he turned.
'This is the Polar district, thou divinst,
Perhaps, as much,' said he. 'The sun thou seest
Shines here much more direct than at the place
Whence thou cam'st hither.' 'Oh ! I see full well,'
I cried ; 'but how I do not comprehend,
Yet would in truth discern? Then he replied :
''Tis part illusion, yet 'tis partly, sole,
And else is real. Since this tract inclines
To the superfices obtains without,
The universal circumflex, it meets,
At equal or approaching incidence,
The solar orb. Here it approaches ; thus,
We have the temperate climate. Let us pass
More inward, there the tropic do we find.
Here the horizon is the zenith half ;
There 'tis itself upon the sunny side.
Yet the horizon's here invisible,
And but obscures the sun when he descends,
Like to a mountain hidden ere that hour,

Or an ethereal cloud that veils compact,
Itself unseen, yond which he passes, as
Behind a frame or solid firmament.
  Yonder the sun is hot, e'n when he sets ;
For such the pow'r of rays direct, they thwart
All else conditions, concentrate their force,
And multiply their numbers thro' the space
In such proportion, none could e'er compute
The vast disparity, and strengthen each.
  But let us farther. There 'tis never day,
The solar day, but yet 'tis always light.
A constant twilight 'twere, did not eclipse
The frequent suns, their far superior blaze
The steadier affluence. These torches form
By mere reflection, are not suns, but yet
Effulgent centres, whence both light and warmth
Irradiate, mock lustres, yet have pith,
Sometimes a single one and numbers oft ;
So modified, belike, the sunny shaft
A rocky height impinges more aslant,
Or lengthened plain, or valley deep a-front :
As when a mirror casts a light, averse
The first direction, quite athwart its pale,
Or as a burning glass adown that brings
The beam to such a focus 'tis a fire,
Nor mere illumination, heat disposed,
That scorches all where'er its fervor turns,
A new creation, elemental pow'r.
  This is the supra-tropic. Never fraught
Albeit the day's light in this far retreat,
Thou couldst not live a moment there impaled,
Save thou wert changed in thy corporeal pulse,
Because of that hot temperature prevails.'
  I interposed at this. 'Yet I would wish
To be informed more fully.' 'And thou shalt
Hereafter be, but thou must be conformed
Still more and more for such contingency.'
My guide announced. Then he proceeded thus :

'These habitants can never pass beyond
The radiant circle. 'Twere as slight for them
To live without, as thee in fire to live,
Or in the water. Here are they as much
Confined as if they dwelt in Jupiter,
Or in the moon. Ev'n less could they exist,
In such an atmosphere as thou hast kenned,
Than ye could in their uttermost, without
A transformation. They would be congealed,
As ye would be consumed, within a glance
Of th' eye's quick time. Full tender are they, soft,
And sensible to most obnoxious cold;
But bear the highest heat with slight ado,
As almost fire-proof; where he would expire
That salamandrine insect they might live.
 Such in the polar day: but when 'tis fled,
And th' equal night her lengthened sway assumes,
'Tis most diverse amid the denizens.
Now, these the most exposed to th' outer winds,
And neighboring th' icy border, tho' remote,
Are dormant like the hedge-hog, or they seem,
So nearly such, one could not say 'twere wrong,
To own the hybernated like that tribe.
 In the interior from th' interior warmed
Are they profuse, nor there the cold winds pierce,
And light scarce less they have than formerly,
From the converging sides reverberate.
The stars are deeper, brighter, and themselves
Repeat, and multiply, and oft replace
As did the orb of day. The lunar beam
Augmented is and oft redoubled casts
A flood of silver radiance to the verge,
Oft as she roams the equatorial line,
Th' ascendant sphere. Together they invoke
A major pyrotechny, grand and full,
Like shivering rockets, now, like massive flames,
Enlarged and splendent if not beautified.
And now the orbs move slow, yet move, and wind

Around the surfaces, pass and repass,
Go and return, extinguish and illume,
And moon-like meteors glow, and falling stars,
And evanescent haloes teem, and melt,
And grow to multitudes, and fade as soon,
Resplendent darkness, if the day unlike.
 Here, too, we've day and night, the light and shade,
Like day and night, when'er the sun is up ;
For as he moves, upon the antipodes
He throws himself, alternate. circling round,
And casts the half obscure, deflected sole
A semi-glance, as when a lumined cloud,
Returns a ray, altho' the source is hid ;
Or as some precipice impending high,
The sunshine intercepts, but yonder marks
The same unmodified, by th' opposite
Ingathered fair, which leaves it crude and dull.
So here, since these are truly such, reversed
The other sides, th' antipodes of each,
The one is lighted up, the other dimmed.
With such precision, too, this course is kept,
They never vary but an eyelid's blink,
This light and shade thro' all the semi-year,
But keep twelve hours exact, an equal guage,
From first to last, and every year that rolls.
 How great variety, thou, then, perceivst,
Of clime we have, of light from day to dusk,
From dusk to darkness, thence, by fitful gleams
Illuminated, like the lightning's stroke,
Now, instant, now, as when the fiery flash,
Midway arrested were, and close at hand,
Remained so luminous the sunshine next,
Oft half the hour, or minutes, from the most
To momentary, thus, essential charge,
And movement ceaseless, more or less, but stayed,
At times, a brief transition, similar,
Now fixed, then vanishing, a pageant framed
Of scintillations passing into gloom,

And thence emerging from the retrospect,
Munificent revolving mutual still,
Single, or manifold, an endless phase.
Nor less diversify the vapors, too,
And have their friendly uses. Here they twine
In rapid exhalations oft, and rise,
And amplify to clouds, till beating rain
Descends and irrigates the drouthy wastes,
And fructifies the fields, and fills the streams,
And renovates the fountains, all refreshed.
And gales replenish too the sluggish air,
And lull to breezes or to tempests grow;
While oft the whirlwind brings destruction down
More palpable than all the wafting winds
Work benison, th' inertia as they fan.'
While thus th' informant spake a vapor fell
In teeming show'rs. We hied to shelter 'neath
An overhanging ledge of jutting eaves.
I was perplexed and cried in doubtful mood.
 'How—if this be like an expanded cave,
Or an interstice in the mundane bulk—
How do these waters run, as I observe,
Not down, but upward, and the rolling floods
Speed outward to the ocean, 'stead toward
The centre, from it; likewise do these rains
Fall perpendicular upon the ground
Whereon we stand, whereas 'tis not the base,
But side precipitous of that vast void,
Which far the elsewhere rounded mass indents,
'And how, too, do we cling, inverted odds,
In such a mode to such descending holds :
Oh! give me clue, my guide, for I am blind?'
Thus I exclaimed, confused; then he returned :
 'Perchance, thou deem'st it as a miracle,
Naught less than such, but be advised, 'tis not.
Nature accomplishes, to steady laws
Accordant, these provisions, full as well,
As elsewhere she subserves an ordered end.

'Tis in excess here the relations are,
Which makes it wonderful to note the like,
And more than wonderful, apparent guise.
　Each compound hath its kernel, and each core
Its centre, to which all the circle throbs,
And all the emanations still recur;
And where a mass from still a greater mass
Becomes detached, its own dependence finds
The sattelite, the planet or the mote.
Here are these promontories: far and vast,
They bulge beyond the earth's proportions else,
Half separate or more than half, and shun
The central pow'r in part, nor coalesce,
In the configuration of the sphere,
Conformally, compacted as the wont,
Whence, so imperfect moulded to the form
Their own attraction supersedes, at last,
The far more distant, sensible above
The other, th' inner globe itself averse,
Predominant. And thence 'tis gravity,
That presses to the mass directly prone,
Ev'n here as otherwhere, and naught exacts
Unusual, or not tenable round the world:
In brief, to each rotundiform it weighs
Invincible, where'er the same is met,
Ev'n on that verge toward the ice, till turns
Our circling countenance diverse itself,
Its former attitude, where stand we, now,
And at an angle to it sole erect.
　Why these sole contraries do not exist
Without this deep depression, when thou cam'st
This way, their counterpart, it is. because
Th' attractive influences there coincide.
Concentric, and the sweep is more abrupt
Within the concave, shaping to its use,
Then at the convex on the frame without.
　Yet, let me not pass by, what yet there lacks,
What yet would lack of perfect order, this

Is still by a magnetic force supplied,
Which thus corrects the slight, divergent bent,
And what imperfect is turns straight and whole,
And like a safety-valve the balance keeps
'Tween oscillations, that would else disturb
The equilibrium 'mid the natural pow'rs
And large appliances less nicely weighed,
And oft erratic from the incidents
They meet, not synchronous, and out of joint,
Or not complete, which then this effluence holds
In its embrace and makes the concord sure.
  Let me explain, again, and more enlarge
So thou shalt have no scruple. Thence it comes,
That the Magnetic Pole th' explorers found,
Erst as they labored in the Arctic wilds,
Where the charmed needle drops and comes to naught,
Is thus deflected from the spheral Pole,
Because of this diversity of shape,
And this eccentric void of bulk and weight,
This non-conformity of orbic needs :
But as th' exception is, nor bears dispute,
So is the balanced means that all befits.'
  ''Tis strange,' I interrupted. 'Strange !' he said,
'Strange—the phenomena are novel, but
The law is common thro' the universe.'
  He then continued : 'If thou'rt dubious still
Of these mere properties, which at a glance
Are not perceptible, soon as thou cam'st,
To where these variant tendencies do meet
And merge together at the terminal node,
And then recede, thou'lt have more evidence,
An ocular solution pried, at once,
That leaves thee no altern'tive but t' admit.
The perpendicular thou'lt find to lean,
On either side toward the other sloped,
Tho' quite erect, and with thy virtual eyes
Wilt mark the like past cavil whence thou lookst,
Or from the actual centre or the sides,

And thou thyself wilt at an angle stand
To all that is not on the very spot,
Apparent to thee and not to be denied."
  He ceased, and vanished from my former note
Insensibly. I sank into a stoop
Of lethargy, oblivious half, absorbed.
Methought, thereafter, 'twas incipient change,
Which on me triumphs, and I was thus transformed
In slow gradation quietly prepared
Ev'n as my guide had omened ere he fled,
For the emergency to go beyond.
  Soon waking now restored on facile wheels,
As with the flight of wings, I far was borne
Around the contiquities, enwrapt,
And halting, here and there, to ponder oft,
Was opportune to mark the region's traits,
And native products and climatic fruits.
  No vegetable growth is like the rest
Of the sublunar, found in other parts ;
The type of them, their individual sorts
Not even, are they oft. Ev'n here, along
The tempered latitude diverse they prove.
The grasses are, but not the same ; the trees
Deciduous are, with scarce an evergreen,
But widely differ in their germs and leaves.
'Tis doubtful, were they evermore allied
With those without, or would those turn to these,
From the seed nurtured, scarce the bud would live.
The flow'rs are vari-formed, but have their hues
More luminous, as with redoubled light ;
The fruits are esculent by those indwell,
Full oft, but scarce were such to tastes above.
Or whether are there essences and salts,
Within the atmosphere or in the earth,
Distinct from them obtain in other climes,
That work these differences, since still the soil
Is equal, and the vaporous plight the same,
Would need a guide t' inform to full effect.

Palms are there in the tropics, stately palms;
But here ungenial crops or poisonous pulps,
They bear prolific. Tho' not vinous, vines,
That ripe hard nuts, while berries grow in pods;
And lentiles fill with drupes, the stead of beans,
And oft pomaceous from the husk depend,
Like to large apples seeming only such,
As bearing likeness to what elsewhere thrives,
And yet so contrary one could not think;
As 'twere designedly an opposite
Amid resemblance, or a mockery
Of th' earth's circumference, its settled modes.
Placed farther, now, what teeming wonders strike
The mute perception! There the verdure grows
Nocturnal hued, with scarce a sunny shade,
To touch th' engarniture so vastly fraught,
Egregious waste of umbrage, succulent
And dank, that foot of man could never wind,
Save where, at times, the aborigines
A pathway fells, or makes a resting place
And shelter from the hostile whirls and rains.
There oft the leaves are boughs, and single-fruits,
The heart of spacious stems, that bear no more,
And larger than the undivided trunk,
Whose rind is like a house, a door each bud.
Where all the undergrowth is matted thick,
A wilderness of mushrooms' sudden growth,
But ne'er to mould, and strongly, massive framed,
Gigantic canopies and bulbous roots,
Near indistructible and firmly knit
With inter-twining tendrils, too profuse,
And shutting out the glimmering lamps, that round,
Orbicular, the nightly as the day's.
Such is the herbage, too, in shooting spires,
Fugacious oft, but doubly fraught and quick.
   The bloom is dark, or only wears a tinge
Of vari-color, so to make them seem
Like enamel, a marvel, while they cease,

Ev'n as the solar lumination fades.
To gloom within the circuit, tho' without
The sun still shines and Summer hither leads.
  My guest was for the animals, I saw
Such single specimens, as were full odd
From all that I remembered. Now I marked
A gentle inmate at my side, to whom
I spoke appealing, and he understood,
Significant, my gesture, pointing out
Some else varieties, from which I learned
There were such classes as the quadrupeds,
The reptiles, with the insects and the tribes,
Vermicular, but winged birds were rare,
And most the feathery bipeds walked without
Their embryo pinion's usefulness displayed.
Else had they no similitude to speak
Quite otherwise, the snakes were round, as oft
As elongated. Oh! what horror struck,
To view them venomous like blight itself!
Yet they were not so harmful as they seemed,
I was advised. What myriad insects, too,
Of sorts diversified; what noisome shapes,
Ev'n from their first appearance one would shrink,
As from the plague! Yet they but threatened thus,
And are much gentler than they signify.
But here I noted one among the beasts,
Which are not plentiful and few the sorts,
The semblance tho' remote an elephant's,
Yet larger still in amplitude, but lacked
His lower limbs, whene'er he moves he crawls,
And finds enough without his going far,
And to defend himself his pouch he spews
A deadly poison all that's hostile near,
As tho' a landed whale so fierce he spouts.
  Receding now to th' outlet, here they grow
Less preternatural in feature still.
These inter-earthly products, more allied
To those on th' outward sprung tho' ne'er the same.

There come th' audacious birds in flocks, at times,
And variegate the welkin high abroad,
The only living tribes from th' outer world,
That ever round the icy barrier aught
Or e'er revisit here from age to age—
The swans with most their colder conginers,
The gulls with theirs, the mallards manifold.
　I was transported thence, and underwent
A gradual change, returning. Now a trance,
As 't were, again enfolded me ; I grew
Forgetful, dumb, and now devoid all sense,
When waking slow I found me here i' th' ship,
Transferred, transformed, and what I was before."
　Thus Moulton. All his mates astonished heard,
And Lyman pausing yet, at last began :
　"Hear ye such news?   Or probable or not,
But visionary, or a devious dream,
'Tis not impossible ; nay, oft there are
Such instances as cannot be gainsaid,
And prove most notable such mighty things
Are there, to be revealed, to comprehend.
But think'st thou, Moulton, this was more than sleep
Brings, mere illusions of the wandering brain,
So oftentimes, which hath no serious weight?"
　"Whate'er the medium which enwrought the spell,
As clear as it now is my vision was,
What I beheld was real, I have no doubt
The least, 'twas true, and what I was informed,
Here the true Hyperboreas duly dwell."
　"Then thou wilt be the last of us to shrink
If any be first, last, from making sure
Th' experience which thou hadst, and proved to all
The frail or veritable, whether found
Thro' vaporous fancy but, or truths inspired."
　"I am most ready, 'tis my foremost wish."
Thus mutual they ; then all went to their berths.

BOOK VI.

PILGRIMAGE PURSUED AND ENDED.

Congenial to all tribes the summer comes.
Him welcome all. In the Arctic e'en he brings
Fresh expectation and rejuvenate joys.
Day hath his fullness, and he fills, alone,
The constant aspect circling th' azure void,
And grown to stature from his infant birth
Down the meridian. Th' icy thraldom breaks
In many a vale, and feels itself dissolved,
Or rudely shaken, all the chain disrupt;
At which indignant groans, and roars, and storms
The invaded solitude and tyrant frame,
The binding bolts unhinged and wrenched apart,
In whose upbraiding turmoil gather skill
The living, and the deadened oft awake
In torpor buried. Now its taken gives
The hazy mildness how the pith's disturbed,
That thrilled the winter, and in sicklier hues
Than e'er have count'nance when the frost is flush,
His dying agonies the rime proclaims.
  Oh! ye Favonian airs, ye midland calms,
Come hither and transport us, least a-while!
The summer reigns, the partial summer calls
To freedom from this bondage worse than night's,
To light from long imprisonment relieved;
Light's restoration and the warmth's relief,
Hail, let us sing, ye powers, high and great,
Once more recurring t' back the halting theme,

The Pilgrims of the Pole again resume.
　So oft unwonted obstacles prevent
The already enterprise when nearest rife,
And in its increment portend defeat :
But not so now with them, the aidful means
Concomitant, and tending to one aim,
The busy crew preparative are sped,
True to th' expected hour, th' appointed time
Nor lags, nor hastens them ; they take their course.
The polar petrel leads and goes before,
As tho' to signify their forward march,
Precarious oft, but not to be declined,
And to embolden them, invited, thus,
The harbinger of hope, a friendly guide,
In that express direction they intend,
He soars above, and beckoning them to go.
　Now they depart, and leaving their stronghold
A slender quota from their number filled,
Not unacquainted with the perilous path.
Onward—a cheerful entrance in the suit
Of followers where none led, bestows them cheer.
The icy pallisades the shore that guard,
Their spacious breadth they travel, swift at first,
On gliding sledges drawn, but soon are hemmed.
Pent up, they now invest, surround, surmount
The Humboldt glacier ; stem the dizzy glare,
And steepled pinnacles beleaguer oft,
To wind them circuitous, which so they must,
And lengthen thus the way, the time exhaust.
But they prevail, intrepid host, they leave
The steepy dams, the glittering crests behind ;
At hairbreadth risk they hang upon the glades,
Fallacious sliding, sloping to betray,
With all their burdens cast upon their care,
Yet conquer safely, and the march proceeds.
　Ah, well-a-day ! the bold manœuvre lasts,
And other difficulties they o'erpass
Successful, like to these, tho' oft repelled,

Again, besieging till the portal pierced,
They make their way unfearing, undeterred!
And oft delay they must for weary miles
To make a circuit, where they breast a gorge
To penetrate the height, or round the gulf,
Or overcome the lower barrier, yet,
That else impregnable defies their toil.
   Would ye go, whither? Ah, where would ye halt,
Ye fearless company? Now, they mount up
A glacial ridge, a ridge, the last of such,
The last of th' Arctic Highlands, which forbids
The wanderers to enfilade it, or front,
And press the shore a-foot. A gibbous horn
Projecting wide, it spurns them from the face
Of the anterior to the abyss edge,
And leaves them no resource but still to climb.
   They mount, they move, and reach the acme, stand
Upon the summit, now. Lo! there behold
The open, iceless sea, O joyful view!
Th' immeasured ocean moved, whose fluctuate waves,
Rise, fall and languish like the fervent South's,
Which far the plumaged races decorate,
Sweeping on high, wild ducks and pelicans,
And briny cormorants that feed on fish.
A home-like scene; how much the glance reminds
The pilgrims of their own and native coast,
So recent theirs, it needs not to affirm!
But to their own reality they come,
Full soon restored, where they are now, and what.
Upon the verge they are, and at the end,
Confounded men, and finished is their task.
They meditate and stand as 'tween two worlds,
In the ethereal vacuum; rigid, stern,
And fettered fast, but bright and crystaline,
The one this side; the motive world of change
Terrestrial, the liquid counterpoise,
And the earthly plenitude of shores and skies,
On th' other, far receding, endless stretched.

Their onward travel's o'er; the latent Pole
Is yonder, o'er the billowy waste secure,
Impassable except to stormy ships;
And here the coast is low and trends away
Quite opposite, and meets the refluent tides
Half toward the noon. The bridging ice that spans
The evening's distance there indefinite,
Serene transparency, that radiates
The crystal deeps, the skies, the glassy plain,
Is now a shining beach, that spurs and spurns
The crazy breakers; now receives the surge,
Then casts it back, disdainful as itself,
That howls discomfited, and turns within
Its own enormity to find amends.
 Nor long they linger, now; they turn their backs
As in offended guise upon the scene,
And from the lofty esplanade descend.
At first 'twas cheer, a sudden-memoried joy;
But next, mere disappointment, such a phase
Was out of place there, and they yet preferred
The everlasting chain that bound them fast
In th' icy revelry, that had no term
Or soft dismissal for the terror-tied.
As when some mariner arrives the port,
He gladdens first, and owns a timely bliss;
But soon he tires, and wish's again to roam
The wavy danger, more himself he feels
On the habitual billows, else at fault,
To rove, save momentary, and hates the stay
From th' element by destiny consigned,
Unless at his own earlier home delayed,
Indigenous, and where he stops, at last,
Prolonged, and seeking only there repose,
He finds it satisfied, nor more he stirs,
Sole haven there more welcome than the sea;
So they, congratulating to return,
Far hasting, to their ice-imprisoned ship.
Fastidious fastened; 'tis their final choice.

Their well-advised return, what now assails
With threatening ills? Alas, the wily bears
Have plundered and destroyed the wary cache,
At proper interval deposited,
Unwary still, forsooth? For what shall ward
Their strength immense, and keenest appetite
For luscious viands, once they scent their trace?
The heavy boulders rolled at distance safe,
The savory hoards are empty, broken down
The canisters, and not a crumb is left
Of all the precious store, their wearing strength
Still to replenish, there so careful stowed;
Till near privation bodes t' afflict them sore,
Ere at their destined distance they arrive.
  The more they haste, and fortunate arrear,
The buxom ptarmigan they plenteous cross,
Successive game, and still successful get.
He furnishes nutritious, fresh supplies;
He mends their want's immediate, keen appeal,
Till the next station hails. His winter white,
The summer hues to brown; already, now,
His plumage turns discolored, on the crest
The feathers mottled, soon his vest is worn
A darkened cincture, none would know him like.
  At last is visible the kindred cape.
They near their refuge. Now, the blatant clouds
Forgather wild, nor only bluster theirs.
Vociferous first, portentous piled, they grow
To swifter violence, soon, terrific-drive,
A hurricane, which sweeping, falls upon
The smooth, hard plane; none can withstand the blast,
None stand before its might, its fury stem,
And all are prone, still happy can they cling,
And are not flung aloft, or witless rolled.
Well for them t'ard the firm land blows the storm.
Yet one among them glides adown the front
O' th' glancing, pending pier, caught by a nook,
And lands upon a floe not there to bide.

Too soon dislodged, the slippery floe affords
Not ev'en a hold. He merges in the floods,
O'erwhelmed and buffeted, but, quick release,
Is hurled upon another icy plat,
Thence to the lower shore is whirled along,
Where it descends to th' edge, devoid a wall,
And pillowed up, not either beat to death
Or only drowned, yet scarcely still alive,
Till rescued by his comrades; he is saved,
A marvel near, tho' but the rarest hap.
 All hail the restoration! Nipped by the ice,
Nipped by the gilded waves, chilled by the thaws,
Th' unyielding or dissolving snows, they've here
Abundance still. They know where'er the hunt
Is most auspicious, where the reindeer halt,
And th' oft seals harbor, to refresh their sorts
Of stored provisions and hale change supply:
They lack not those and these bestow them zest
And health promoted, while their means they add.
 All hail, a fly! Whence comest thou, frail dupe,
Or art thou not a dupe to this fair sun
And shining weather? Or art thou native bred,
And couldst thou bear th' interminable Frost
Enduring endless, not being sacrificed
By his fierce certitude and ceaseless blight?
Thou hadst perforce an envious shelter thine,
A most uncommon, such as sole thou found;
Thence thou'rt alone. Nay, thou couldst never brave
The turpid cold in thy mete embryo wrapped.
Thou art a wanderer. Ah! thou wert beguiled,
So far away from where thou hadst thy birth,
So far from thy companions, by thyself,
'Mid the celestial promise of the day.
How could thy gauzy pinions ever waft
Thee so remote from thy congenial haunts,
Nor they dismembered by the pinching rime!
Or the mere weight of flight the thousand miles,
Such feeble membranes! Know, thou'rt not a bird,

To cleave the ether ; yet thou'rt here, indeed,
Then welcome thee, rare visitant, be thou
Invited tho' admonished, lauded, too.
But dost thou bide—ah, thou will be impierced
By the returning sharpness ! Oh, thou'lt be
Swift at an hour sore stricken, seared thy wings,
Thy flexile wings, and thou'lt lie low, death-stilled.
Haste then, fly thence, retrace thy winnowing track,
Soon as thou mov'st to some more sure retreat
In warmer bowers less fickle, nor to clip
Thy plumes reticulate, and beauteous limbed :
But now be welcome—ah, the summer's child ?
  As when some once acquainted stranger meets
The traveler in far lands, where all are strange,
Naught valued then, he now becomes a friend,
And welcomes glad. What once had been a task
Is now a pleasure, and he entertains
Him kindly, but the more so highly prized,
Because of all the loneliness so fraught,
And the encounter, novel and unweened :
So likewise, as the embolded creature sits
His feet on Lyman's glowing cheek indulged,
He does not brush him thence, but leaves at peace,
Encouraging, till at his own accord
So to depart he choose, and is rejoiced.
  But, now, to flatter them no leisure's theirs.
Let them be up and doing, too brief a turn,
The while the season favors ; soon it fades,
And scarce begins it teeming 'tis cut short.
  Soon as recovered from th' inert fatigue
Of th' erst adventure, forth they fare, improved
And hardened to th' endeavor, stronger stead
More weakened by the rigorous Arctic's lull.
  They start their fleeting teams, alert, now by
The West-land, moving sanguine to the chase,
So hopeful, since they've reason, for a clue
They'd found already, and here they may advance
Beyond the confines, which before had curbed

Inopportune, their progress farther out.
They thwart the channel, an unbroken belt
Of solid flood t' invisible degrees,
Stretches invulnerable from shore to shore.
How swift their speed upon the smooth expanse!
But now 'tis labor 'mid the partial thaws
And marshy snows, upon the reeking land;
Yet they wend cheerful, such they knew, at first,
And 'tis not all incumbrance, nor the chill.
  Inordinate the skies in drizzly mists
Grow dreary, now, and mystify the sun.
The vapors thicken and t' expansion teem
O'er all the hemisphere, and turn to rime,
And soon the tiny flakes a myriad host
Show'r down munificent and wrap the realm.
As yet 'tis calm, but soon the sweeping storms
Awake impenetrate, and wildly wail
Their hungry dirges o'er the dulled expanse.
Now the fall amplifies, and volumes roll
O'er the unfilling earth adown the maze,
And darkness cumulates, e'en in midday
As 'twere the night. The driving tempests scud
Impetuous-whirled and cast the fleecy hoards
In overwhelming piles, can none escape,
Or battle with save at incongruous odds.
  Hath he returned? The savage winter howls.
He will not yield his empire easy won,
Without a struggle, or shall yield at all.
Does he take up the reins and conquering rides,
And beats the sunshine back no more to smile,
Defeated, and its short-lived memory broke?
His pow'r resumed, nor once more put to flight?
  So now portends he. Yet, a sudden spell,
Perchance 'tis only, vanished soon as ris'n,
Such here th' uncertain skies, and like a wolf
Amid the peaceful folds, may Boreas come.
Ev'n in midsummer, his despite to breathe,
Shut up the sun, and vanquish summer's self,

Awhile, at least. Capricious as the gales
The balmy welkin is, and soon may sink
Into mere wintriness, and put on gloom
Most suddenly, the kindling warmth's surprise
And blasting bane, will not be quite repulsed.
　Yet this invasion's 'yond the rigor's wont.
The while the time two double days and nights
Encompasses, the deep impulsion falls,
Naught intermitting and augmenting vast,
Abyssmal plains, and heights like mountains heaped,
The ceaseless drifts upbearing build immense.
The lapsing pilgrims flounder 'mid the flare,
And come to counsel. Cries the leader loud—
The drift is louder still, he scarce is heard
Yet understood, a gesture guides as well—
" Return," " return," where'er a voice remains.
　Long had they striven forward but in vain ;
And should the avalanche at last surcease .
It still would baffle them. They could not pierce
Th' abounding tumult e'en when laid to rest,
So many leagues, 'mid sheer exhaustion lost,
Or least disabled, rescue ne'er to know,
And keen starvation threatening, what wer't else
Than madness to persist ; they must return.
Ev'n now 'tis doubt if that desirous end,
The refuge from these weird entanglements,
They may accomplish and arrive, secure
Their lives and limbs, where only they can pause.
　Along the wind-swept gulleys they deploy,
And by the sinuous light, where yet the waves
Are liquid and absorb the flushing snows,
Nor leave a shallower path, they retrograde.
But ofttime a continuous ledge obstructs,
Thro' which they needs must scoop their blinding track,
Unconscious half, and strangled half, and deaf,
Each hid from th' other, and unknown a space,
Till on the emptier span they dimly meet.
　But one is missing now ; a sailor lacks,

Nor yet emerges. Then they beat about,
Assiduous winding 'mid the shifting deeps.
They call with might ; none answers, none appears,
And all is silent save the tempest's sough.
And now, th' imperious bounty threats t' enclose
Them, where they wait or delve, not envious gifts
To lend them evident, but to death thrall,
And suffocate them 'mid the drowsy banks,
Th' ungracious result surely ; they must on,
And leave their comrade to uncertain fate,
Whom never more they see or find to live.
 How shall they speed or e'er survive, themselves ?
A common day's extent the drift they brave,
When lo ! the sky breaks out, the rolling clouds
Disperse precipitate, and leave them light
And kindly calm to thread the plumy heights !
What joy the sunshine is ! if oft before
They welcomed it as nature's brightest, best,
'Tis now a treble grace, and glads them through,
Above whate'er its advent yet had wrought
In all their days, or memory yet revived !
 Ev'n now 'tis difficult to make their way ;
But soon they come where th' urgent breakers stop,
To silence chilled, and th' icefoot gives them room,
Denuded oft by th' overpow'ring winds
To bareness, and accessible to speed,
Ere half an hour. Yet, ere the quickened road
They occupy, within a sheltered reach,
But swept clean-besomed from the showery flakes,
Which haply they'd encounter, there they build
A depot, such provision they can spare
Undoubting, now, to store for future wants,
Which ne'er they forfeited, but carried past
All hard emergencies, the while unknown
Their coming prospects, where to come or halt :
Thus, disencumbered too more free they move.
 Nor did they now the next advance neglect,
Tho' thus shut up as tho' forever pent

From the up-polar march, and such defeat,
Ev'n ere they measured but the vestibule
Of the Pole's entrance ; as determined, now,
As ever to go thitherward, they'll try
An else occasion, so provide the means.
Foreseeing, and well husbanded, the while :
O'er all the hoard they raise a rocky cairn,
Well fortified, t' attack beseeming proof.
  Onward awhile—and on the frowsy flakes
Fain would they slumber, now, while mantle-wrapped,
Some couch recumbent down, so sorely spent.
But better heed upwakes them : "on"—they shrill,
" No hour to loiter here." Thus, yet they march.
And now the portage hails them where they crossed,
And now will cross the channel : th' icy belt
Is firm as ever, sure 'twould not dissolve
'Mid th' ice-winged element, the more congealed.
  Full forwardness they've here, and scarce provokes
Them one impediment, these vapors whelmed.
On the glazed surface they like feathers glide
Before Euroclydon, hurled to the gulf
Above, below, within the watery isles
And liquid labyrinths the space that fill :
The path is clear full well, they've but to go.
  Ere yet they stir, a brace of worried dogs
Lie dead before them on the silent beach,
And moveless, now, too much, too long beset
By the unwearied snows, they sank and died,
And there they stretch the mazy mould amid :
Old, but experienced, none were better aid
In the enterprise—Grim, Growler were their names.
  Joy for this last relief, they would have fall'n,
Lost and to perish 'mid the murky maze,
From the too long detention wrought to waste,
And the necessitous and reckless strife,
Unceasing, and the lack too long of rest :
Now at their cabin halt they glad but faint.
Of their escape, so provident, at last.

To dally with the time is signal loss,
So soon the season's o'er wherein to reap.
Again, they journey, soon as fitly nerved
T' exposure and to hardihood restored ;
But less they need provide, their numbers less,
And less their teams to carry, surer speed.
Some are disabled yet, and some to guard
The stately brig must stay, the more expert
And buoyant are selected for the jaunt.
  But what before they 'scaped, delays and mars
Them various, now, the need to cross the wave,
Their footing reft. The solid girdle 's rent ;
The icebergs farther move, the floes impinge
And clash together. So they man their barge,
And ship their double sledge therein, and 'tween
The dangerous reefs and shivering glaciers run,
And steady them upon the icy fields,
At times, or cut their progress thro' the block.
  Unharmed they make the shore ; the favoring tides
Facilitate. They tread their former course.
The recent snows are fled, and naught prevents
Their haste to forward. Ere the dripping banks
They leave behind, their boat they bury there,
And mould protective round the same a cairn ;
For should this fail them on their coming back,
How should they reach their quarters evermore !
So much they venture, yet the risk abridge
Thus provident ; for Christiansen declares,
If any natives yet these regions haunt,
'Tis unaware, none know. If so, but build
This mound, so like 'twill be, as did they not,
As tho' they were not live, untouched ; they ne'er
Will broach a cairn, 'tis sacred in their eyes.
Besides their mates have orders, and agree,
Who in the ship remain, within a month
Should lack their presence and no word from them.
Perchance they may in other boats they've left,
Cruise 'mid the bergs and frozen breakers clear,

To seek them out, and find their way is shut,
And bring them back, if so, that never else
Had once returned, condemned to wander lone
On icy brinks, where none remove or lodge,
Or meet their destitution, or a shield
From sheer destruction all the wild affords,
Or modes to meet their comrades, they to find.
  Such is their venture, nor the shapely ship
Will they allow to move, that ne'er could wait
Were they but missed, nor e'er return could make
Once were it loosed, but must go on to port
Such as may hap, or out the open sea,
Or break to piecemeal fragments, doomed a wreck
Unmitigated, and without release.
  Advance they cautioned, thus, with every phase
Indulgent to their most abounding wish.
  Ho! th' open ocean, now, they hail in view!
High-hearted they proceed, and far as first
They were, beyond, in latitude arrive.
The ice-foot fails them first; the surges lash
The beaten shores. Now gather up the clouds;
Now they disperse, th' aerial vistas fair.
Now they assemble wide, and drenching rains
Descend, instead the later-driving snows.
Now storms arise and wane. Now fleeting mists
Enwrap the heights, white-robed, in silvery shrouds,
Or azure-hued in flowing mantles clad,
Enfold the mountains and approach the skies.
Now quick, brief show'rs of pelting hail deform
The clear cerulean, and soon they flit
Away, diminished, or consigned to naught.
Thus every oft vicissitude they feel,
Still onward, and propitious hopes invite.
  Graced by the constant day, an equal pace
They keep with him; at noon the verge he skirts
Of the horizon, farther as they wend.
  Now th' o'er-impending cliffs extend athwart,
Straight-steeped, and not inclined, and at the base,

Wave-washed, forbid a foot, a vertic wall.
Then fain they climb it, sanguine-limbed and firm,
And now a higher still they mount, with much
Of varying toil. Alas! a loftier 'yond
Expands perverse, and near invis'ble runs!
They beat about and seek some hidden clue,
Impassable—and none the top may scale,
They find it surely. Lo! the spreckled loon
Soars high in sight, and far abroad he shrieks,
Of their discomfiture, as tho' a sign,
And to proclaim their ineffectual guest!
They reach their desert height, that too they leave,
Turn back, the dazzling eminence away,
With much chagrin. Yet, could they more, in truth;
As well to grieve they cannot climb the moon?
The Northern diver tells the Pole intact.
They grieve, but not despairing, far they trod,
And needs their means exhausted, must supply
Them farther; little farther could they go,
Were the way open, save they fill their fare.
 On, to a deeper promontory climbs
Th' intent commander. There, beyond the front
Of the stupendous precipice, recede
The heights still lower, undefined and far,
How far, who knows? To know is not for them.
 Not less than when some warrior moves against
A place entrenched, and wins a signal breach,
But sees dismayed an inner rampart rise,
Far stronger than the first, and in its stead,
While all his best resources swallowed up;
Unequal to the contest, now, perforce,
He draws away thence, sad, and sorely vexed—
Not less is Lyman foiled. But famine threats
Ev'n now, to compass them; the teams have lack
Of provender, and will have more full soon.
No animals are here except the seals,
To fledge the hunt. "There, there they do resort,"
Says Christiansen. But who will wait for them?

Haply for days they must, who seek, ere yet
They do appear, and then a scanty score,
At last, they yield, far less by many a weight,
Than do the greedy dogs meantime devour.
  See, where the wild geese breed among the crags :
The land birds and the water-fowl their homes
Have in the precipices, and they build
Their nests in dizzy fronts, from whence they scan
That fish the sea, their prey in deeps below.
The wary gull disports, and on the wing
Perceives his enemy, and stoops to clutch ;
In shining numbers far he fans and flecks
The void, and dazzles all the atmosphere.
But these are unattainable, prepared
So illy for the game, far else their search,
Who there are roaming. Now they turn their backs,
Half discomposed, not gloomy, to the bound ;
Half-gladdened, too—they did a space retrieve—
And leave the glittering eminence, afar,
Unseen, or hidden from the distant view.
  Hails, now, the night, a shortened hour, but fair
As twilight's earliest ; all the stars are dim.
'Yond seems a nebulae of vapid gloom,
Grows like a dusky bank that oft subtends,
At base, th' auroral flashes, 'tween the earth
And skirting sky, along the circuit drawn.
The water-sky, they know it, that which gives
The open water's promise to the south,
And fairer transit heralds o'er the wave,
Than favored, coming ; hopeful they proceed.
  Grateful they find their buried barge unharmed,
And disinter it speedy, giving thanks.
But now the ices cluster thicker by,
And swifter they impinge than when they came.
Thence t'ward the sun to go they soon resolve,
Still farther, where the wrecks from the icy belt,
Are less profuse and massive borne dispersed :
So they believe full certain, th' omens tell.

Perchance, full half an hundred leagues they wend,
Still less the frozen fields, the floes, the bergs,
But yet abounding. Half their famished dogs
Are on the road defunct at varied points;
They can withstand the frost, but must have food,
And scarce the store suffices them that drive,
Much less the herds, whom what remains must serve.
The more their labor is, since on the sledge
Their boat is shipped, and they must pull, full oft.
Save when the floods are fair, they launch their craft,
And paddle by the inward shores, relieved
Their fraughtest burden, thus, betimes, afloat.
   Rest they bestow themselves this side a cape,
Rounding slight distance, here, a slender bay.
Waked, as the sun the circling mist surmounts,
They rise, their progress to resume prepared.
A step—they halt; some graves their note attract,
Not such the natives build, such as themselves
Would consecrate a slighter sepulchre.
   A-while they ponder, silent; some diverge
A trivial space. There Theobald arrests
The present prospect, and he forward bends
In earnest attitude, as one absorbed
In melancholy thought, and yet surprised.
He points beyond with willing finger, though
Unwilled, intuitive, nor once withdraws
His marked attention still. Lyman perceives,
And soon approaches, query in his glance.
"Turn thitherward thine eyes around the knoll,"
Calmly says Theobald in lowly words,
"What seest thou?" Corpses all around are strewed
In numerous numbers; by the tide of years
The skeletons are bleached. How came they there?
'Tis not their ken to answer, while thrice ten
They count them scattered. They were pilgrims, too,
The remnants of their pilgrimage attest.
Cords, bandages and fragment arms,
The locks and stocks of guns in pieces proved,

And special glasses in their parts detached,
Are mingled with the bones. And here beside
Are workmen's relics, carpentry, and mounds,
And stone embankments, such as men would make
To shield them temporary, and only could
Amid the frozen hour, or to outfit
Their worn effects and means to travel 'yond.
And farthermore they find a ship's name carved,
The "Resolute," with yet a single trace
Of a strange name, unknown, an officer's,
On shapely sticks ; but not a record else,
Or date, or effigy, saying whence or where.
 'Twas their last stage, and haply found they here
Final starvation. How could they become
Their seldom nutriment, the covert game,
Amid the piercing, cold vicissitude,
The wint'ry night, or most abbreviate day?
Still less they could, could they have traveled on.
Mayhap they trod too late the farther North,
And here were fastened by the snowy storm ;
Or their good hold, the battered ship, was crushed
By the conflicting frost's o'erpowering force,
And moving battlements, and onset fierce ;
No shelter and no food, they freeze or starve.
 Here was a veteran, perchance, that hoped
From the hard venture, a sufficiency
To gather for the following days of life,
And soothed retirement needing naught averse.
Here a bold youth, his parent's joy and pride,
That long awaited, seasons, days and months,
His coming, crowned with honors and rewards.
Here a fond father with a competence
Returning, his own fireside sought to glad,
And so was sanguine. There his scions bloom
On far-off shores, expectant he arrives,
To make their comforts fuller and complete ;
And there his bosom's mate in anxious tears
Looks for him hourly, seeking why he stays

So long belated, thinking yet he comes,
And brings the wherewithal to feed her flock,
And timely obviate their pressing needs.
  None are redeemed, most like; here all succumb:
Here all their purpose or ambition ends.
What have they, then, for all their wondrous pains?
They ventured, might have won; they dared the lot.
The great pursuit atoned for what they paid,
And more than less pursuits with less of cost,
Atoned it, tho' they sank in sorest wise.
'Twas worthy, tho' the desert only theirs;
'Twas worthy, tho' the solitude alone
Was of them cognizant, and knew their straits,
And their complaint the silence only heard:
Equivalent, tho' short what they deserved,
'Twas something still; the great pursuit atoned.
  Here they embark, the cape a furlong past,
Nor longer will their transit o'er put off.
Quickly and fair the favoring breezes waft
The viewless landing to o'er the open floods;
Tho' yet the ices break in creeking jars,
And crowd together, resonant and rash,
In many a vortex: readily they 'scape
Thro' wider avenues, and reach the land,
Well-timed, and gratulating wield the sledge.
  Scarce have they turned their steps they meet their mates,
Who come to seek them, now a month has lapsed
Since these departed, and had bid them seek
After that interval; on self-same path,
More expeditions thus to cross the brine,
And find them out, where 'twas made choice by these.
  Glad are they met, and yet alike they grieve.
One of their number dies, the furnisher
And waiter of supplies, too weary-worn
And o'er-excited at the present bliss.
They bury him, and raise a mound of stones,
To mark the spot and notify th' event;
Then forward hie, and homefelt soon they climb

The ice-bound ship; tho' solitary, still
They greet it, as from loneliness returned
To wont companionship and welcome home.
  Vain is the polar vision, now, the hope
To reach that utter boundary is by,
No more they'll tempt, the last attempt is made.
And naught they've left but t' extricate themselves
From their environment, pent up, and find
An outlet to the ocean; so return
And leave the Arctic fields before the frost
Grows sterner, and the awful night sets in.
  In vain, alack, that expectation, too!
The brig is prisoned still, without the chain
Is undissevered firm as rock amassed,
And will not break this season, aught of room
T' afford most evident, so early flush
The bitterness, and rigid winds awake.
The new ice forms already, crystals shoot,
Quick clogging o'er the liquid surfaces
In slushes deep. They must remain, alack!
The long, long night, another winter bide!
  Nor this such great mishap; so much they're used
To Boreal influences, them infinite
They might withstand, or longer suffer, but
Their means are slender now, and some are gone.
Their fuel, food, are scant and threat to leave
Them barred enough. These circumstances give
A hue of ill, and their good fare to doubt.
  First, to provide, the stately brig they lift
Up from the depth, to guard her from the shock
And strain of th' ice, abutting. Yet she's free
From rent or dinge, and scarce she owns a wrench,
So oft run foul; they toil to keep her so,
And fix her safe, to be at th' earliest date
Next year, moment offers, firm prepared.
To stem the floods, serene and unalarmed.
  Down to the Esquimaux they speed them next.
For aid in stored provisions, and the food

Of plenteous game. These yield them all they can,
And oft their mutual wants exchange, each t' each,
And oft revisit each, and knit the link
Of friendship stronger, as the wint'ry year
Is riveted more dreadful, mighty and fast :
Else to the Frost themselves resign they, then.
  What here befell them farther, be it passed,
So like domestic cares and famine's ghoul ;
The rats that dwell with them supply a feast.
But worst, the sea-coal wanes ; the ship must yield
Its timbers helpless ; not t' unfit the sail,
And full seaworthiness, all else they spare,
While scurvied ails grow deeper t' ward the Spring.
The Esquimaux, too, starve ; they die of want,
The winter longer, their provision less,
To meet his terrors, for the hunt was scarce.
  Blest Spring, what welcome greets thine opening eye,
Tho' still so lagging ! But the Summer hails
More gladsome, and the pilgrims feel the sun.
  Now they go forth, and watch the meteor void
For gracious signs. The wide, petrific waste
Is harder now than wont, more firmly bound
Than 'twas last season, and they near despair
To get from thence, and e'er the brig dislodge.
Too truly may they ; they explore till late :
No opening offers, near a solid space,
And they must leave the vessel, go alone,
Or bide the wreck to famish or to freeze :
They now resolve, and exit haste t' effect.
  Farewell, thou long-acquainted brig, farewell,
Thou moving bulwark, yet a steady home,
So long a steadfast anchor. Long thou'lt list
The wan, cold winds, the utter waste amid
A solitary beacon, wild and strange,
And there wilt look upon the livid east.
The floods will lave thee while her quartile horn
The moon fulfils, but else the weary ice
Will hold thee fast. Perchance thou wilt emerge

At last beyond thy long-time harbor here,
And stand, a portent, far among the floes.
The dreary storms will visit thee, and thee beat
Full ofttime back; but never wilt be found,
For thrice a thousand miles from hence secure,
As some, thy predecessors in the deeps.
Ah, they'd ne'er pierced these trysting glades so far,
Or proved the frost's ferocity so much,
As thou? At length, thou wilt be torn to shreds,
Or dashed to atoms on the limpid fields,
Or groan thy death-dirge 'mid transcendant bergs,
Too manifold and crowding on thy site.
None, none will rescue thee, thou'lt be alone,
And now thou'rt such, and left to nature's hap,
Wild beating or lone straying, none beseech
Thy preservation or protection now.
Thou wilt go down at last, thou'lt wave no sign,
To warn the solitude thou ere wert there,
And stayed, how long! The night and terror 't last,
Farewell, farewell, the Pole!
Thou'lt be no more.
   By land, or th' ice and water, as befits,
They take departure. Many a slim escape
From near destruction have they, many a mode
Of troublous plight assails, they've t' overcome.
   In midst to th' open sea their distance gone,
They at the native hamlet, Uniah, halt,
They'd known before. There they met Christiansen,
So long away. A weight of Ptarmigam
He brings them thither. "See, my walrus boots
Are worn," he says. "I must again go forth,
And furnish them: when I return to you,
'Twill be beyond with fresh provisions caught."
"Go," answers Lyman; "speed thee well." But ne'er
They saw him more, but heard a maid he wed
Down southward, e'en the while they passed along.
   No farther can Alphonse go; scarbutic ills
Have come to climax. Thrice the sunshine rounds

The Pole, he too is dead, so long they wait,
And make among the friendly natives there
His single tomb, and breathe the last fond pray'r.
Among their faithful allies there he lies.
  Folik and Yocum, too, they meet ; tho' not the first,
'Tis the last meeting. When they go t' unmoor
Their bark, the village all assembles, child,
And man and woman, and such interest prove,
As those who oft their common peril shared.
Values they do exchange and gifts present ;
Those, their superfluous meets, for now their food
Is plentiful, these, furniture, such as
They cannot take, or do not need, and oft
Mementoes for remembrance. Here a sledge ;
One is enough, or more they cannot use,
Or stow the boat, and thus upon the ice
Or land must carry more ; here, too, a gun,
A blanket, knives, and iron, they can spare :
Now stored their craft, them on the shore they leave,
With but one native dog of all their host,
They brought with them above there yet is left.
  One-fourth the year they travel southward borne.
Debarred a roof, in th' open boat, or sledged
On the ice, or march afoot, full oft delayed,
And by the blazoned day scarce less than blind.
Now hail the crimson cliffs, the scarlet snow,
That all the sky beyond rose-colored hues,
In lumined beauty, like th' eternal bloom,
Superlative, that flush's primeval days,
A prodigy th' ethereal amplitude.
Now, the open, feasible sea, no more a ledge
Of binding frost, and but the bergs they hail ;
Or but th' uncrowded icy fields, apart,
And leaving room to avoid where'er they dip,
The waters beautiful, and now adorned
By radiant bergs, and not as late deformed.
  Here their last sledge they leave behind, and take
To seaward wholly. By the terraced steeps

Of Providence they halt, starvation-'scaped.
For here are bounteous birds, the easy auks
Which frantic they devour, how much they want,
They do not know themselves till plenty cheers,
So long at mercy on the billows driv'n,
With but a seal, a rare bestowal, got,
At times precarious, ne'er a full supply.
  Ye kittiwakes, that habit all the heights,
And clothe in liveliness, ye gladden here.
The sun-tipped crystal shines, but ye have room
For your own chambers in the sun-marked rock,
For your own dormitories on the verge
Of falling eminences, in the nooks.
Ye are not food for any, yet ye have
A neighboring multitude, or motes, whose brood
Is edible, and ofttime meet they man,
Or the great cormorant, become a prey.
And yet they flourish e'en as ye, but ye
Escape the snare, ye are more fortunate.
Can ye bestow good omen, O ye birds!
Not fallible, or are ye such, so fair
That populate the heights? Then be the like,
Then do; let prosperous features guide,
Once more, the farthest haven, ye shall plume
Th' aerial spaces, symbol of such hap.
Ye kittiwakes, that hover on the waves,
Tumultuous high above, the desert make
And barren rocks alive, and beautify,
Be ominous, be favorable yet,
Be ye good fortune's sign, that's yet to come!
Such as was still at least, tho' oft disturbed
To close perdition; O ye kittiwakes!
That hover o'er the waves or wing the heights.
  This winter's long night, while the famine raged,
By hunger driv'n or lest their dogs should starve,
Two youths to watch for wolves went on the ice.
They slew one, and the perilous game prepared
Thence to dislodge, when lo! a north wind burst,

And broke the ledge whereon they stood apart
Its continuity? They were adrift,
Nor could they land amid the faithless floes.
What shall they? Now an ice berg do they touch.
They climb it, and with heavy labor draw
Their spoil upon it; yet the sea waves dash
Deep over them. Its higher heights they scale
Ev'n to the topmost. There their canine troop
They lash to knobs, lest by the storm o'erblown,
And bide the reckless danger; flat they cling
'Mid the thick darkness. Now the moonlight throws
Its spell around them, now obscured, and then,
Again, its sheen recovered, while the Frost
Does not indulge them, but their limbs are shred,
Their feet or toes, themselves and animal train,
By the huge creature fed they slew, the while.
A month they voyage. Now the ice berg grounds,
So near the shore, they spy; they may be saved.
They lash themselves and dogs to mutual thongs,
And send them thwart the interstitial floods,
Which draw them over on the crystal floor.
Delivered happily, tho' late, they reach
As risen from the dead their native huts,
So welcomed, ne'er the inmates thought to see
Them more, so long away, their home the berg.
"How came ye thence so far, yet free?" they said.
These answered—"Since we did neglect the rites,
Thence were we punished, and we suffered thus."
For annual, say they, in the hills, and down
The deep glen, come, to Northeast from th' Northwest
The guardian walrus bellows, loud and strong.
The omen cheering is if fair the hunt,
But if 'tis fraudulent betokens ill.
He naught permits his kindred to be slain,
Save consonant to long accepted terms;
Fair dealing sole his guardian voice responds.
Weary man's rest, a rising, jutting ground,
Rounding and halt, the story Lyman lists.

Musing, then, 'gan he thus. Those Esquimaux,
So rugged tho' their realm, and they themselves
So callous to the wild, are yet redeemed
From savage life more facile, and subdued
To gentleness more easily than the rest
Of th' aborigines of this New World,
Nature provides the gracious equipoise ;
The great Creator's laws bring harsh extremes
To equal terms. To close companionship
By the hard temper of the clime constrained,
And the long night, 'tis social life enforced ;
The less its vicinage he can evade,
And from disorder tends he, since so near
The obligation presses on him still.
Tho' so much leisure now, his aptest arts,
Industrial, claim a constant vigilance,
Demand his energies and ordered schemes,
T' uphold existence and his only cheer,
Whence in the desert half he's civilized.
  On, on—the lustrous pathway now they hail
The first for settlement, and greet the Danes.
They gladden entertaining them, and soon
The yearly trader speeds them far apart ;
But the next station meet their novel friends,
Who come to seek them, and they go aboard.
Soon they return whence gone, their locks as white,
All—as the snow they left on th' Arctic fields,
And joy, who wait they greet, the Pilgrims of the Pole.

INDEX.

	PAGE.
BOOK I.—INTRODUCTION, - - - - -	5
BOOK II.—THE VOYAGE, - - - - - -	19
BOOK III.—WINTER QUARTERS, - - - -	33
BOOK IV.—ANGELICAL, - - - - - -	53
BOOK V.—THE DREAM, - - - - - -	69
BOOK VI.—PILGRIMAGE PURSUED AND ENDED, - -	85

www.ingramcontent.com/pod-product-compliance
Lightning Source LLC
Chambersburg PA
CBHW031404160426
43196CB00007B/897